Alchemy
of
Goetia

An Alchemical Study of Grimoiric Sigils

S. Connolly

Alchemy of Goetia

An Alchemical Study of Grimoiric Sigils

S. Connolly

Darkerwood Publishing Group LLC 2024

Darkerwood Publishing Group LLC, Denver, CO

Available In:
eBook
Paperback
Case Wrap Hardcover
Linen Wrap Hardcover
Spiral Bound

Alchemy of Goetia: An Alchemical Study of Grimoiric Sigils is © Copyright 2024 by Stephanie Connolly-Reisner writing as S. Connolly. All Rights Reserved.

No part of this book may be reproduced in any form, electronic or other, without express written permission from the author or publisher. Please respect the authors' copyrights. For more information about the author or demonolatry see:
www.demonolatry.org or www.sjreisner.com

Editorial: M. Blackthorne
Cover: S. Connolly
Interior Design by S. Connolly, M. Blackthorne, and S. Blackthorne
Alchemy Of Goetia

S. Connolly

DB Publishing
An Imprint of Darkerwood Publishing Group LLC

A Word of Warning

Fellow magicians and alchemists, please know that a lot of the recipes and processes described in this book include toxic and volatile substances. By sharing the recipes and processes herein, I am correlating the actual alchemy to the spiritual alchemy based on symbolism, and in **no way** do I recommend or advise that you try any of this. Some of the recipes herein are dangerous in the real-world laboratory setting and could result in bodily harm or death. So be aware of that going in. This book is for reference and contemplation only and should not be used to practice home laboratory alchemy. Or, in laymen's terms, **DON'T TRY THIS AT HOME.** Thank you. – The Author

Table of Contents

Introduction	1
Preliminary Considerations	4
What are Sigils	7
Alchemy	11
Terminology	13
Common Alchemical Symbolism	21
Animals in Alchemy	23
Colors in Alchemy	43
A Key of Alchemical Symbols	48
The Seals of the Goetia	83
Other Grimoires	253
Conclusion	261
Bibliography and Suggested Reading	
Acknowledgments	

Introduction

I first publicly suggested that perhaps the sigils of the old grimoires, in particular – the Ars Goetia (*Goetia* in ancient Greek meaning charm or witchcraft) - weren't just animist depictions of the spirits as insects or creatures, or random characters given to us by the spirits, back when I wrote *Keys of Ocat* in 2012. Instead, I suggested that perhaps within the sigils were encoded alchemical and magical symbolism, giving the magician some additional insight into each Daemonic force/spirit. Possibly even suggesting a process in how the Daemon works, or how one should work with the Daemonic force. I'm not the only magician who has thought this. I know many magicians who've often said that the Ars Goetia "is its own language", to quote a friend. This idea has never left me, and in the years since then, I've searched for books on the subject with no luck. For several years now, I've been studying alchemical and magickal symbolism and the sigils themselves, jotting down my thoughts - as one does.

On the following pages you'll find my musings on comparing alchemical symbols and Goetic seals, and the possible meanings of my findings.

For some of you, this book will be eye opening or give you a new perspective. For others of you, you'll just be excited that you weren't crazy when you saw the same thing, but perhaps never dove into it as deeply as this book attempts to. The western magickal schools of thought are all interconnected, after all.

We have to remember that the first copies of the Ars Goetia appear during the early 17th Century, a time when symbolism, ciphers, and encoded messages were all the rage when it came to hiding esoteric information in plain sight. Alchemy and hermetic thinking were also in fashion among the occultists of the time, meaning the codes would have only been accessible to those initiated into the mysteries. In which case, the sigil characters for each spirit would have been ideal places to hide spiritual alchemical processes, recipes, additional attributes or purposes for each spirit, and quite possibly, even hints for evocation/invocation. Talk about removing the church clothes of the Ars Goetia, right?

Please note that I, in no way, claim that my thoughts on this are gospel or even 100% right. The only person who truly knows 100% for sure what was behind these sigils was the first person to draw them out because it was their personal gnosis to begin with. The rest of us are just speculating. Some have even used these spirit seals, sigils, or emblems in accordance with bio geometry and believe the shapes of the sigils denote a vibrational frequency for each spirit and can help the magician better harmonize with the energy resonance of that particular spiritual or Daemonic force. For all I know, there could be merit to that, but I won't dwell on that here.

Instead, the following pages consist of my subjective musings about the alchemy of each seal. Your interpretation of the seals is entirely your own. Perhaps you'll see symbols or possible interpretations I've missed. Perhaps you'll agree with some points and disagree with others. This book will either give you a new perspective, offer inspiration, or you'll be incensed that I even suggested such a ridiculous idea. That said - do with it as you will. May this book give you inspiration, food for thought, and possibly a different perspective of the Ars Goetia and some other gimoires and their seals.

-S. Connolly, January 2022

Preliminary Considerations

SOME THINGS TO KEEP IN MIND AS YOU PERUSE THIS BOOK:

The symbol(s) for vinegar and acid shows up in a good number of Goetic seals. To the Judeo-Christian trained mind, this would immediately make one think that Daemons are bad since acids are immediately thought of as dangerous as they dissolve physical matter, and vinegars negative due to their flavor and acidity. However, let's take a deeper look at it. Vinegar is also used to clean things and make them sparkle. It can disinfect and deodorize. It can also be added, in small doses, to foods to make them taste wonderful or to preserve food. Acid can be used carefully to remove stubborn substances, to dissolve things - metaphorically dissolving obstacles perhaps. Some acids are useful in digestion or cooking. Others can be used to make consumable items like dye and soaps. Acids, by their chemical nature, are neutral because they contain the same number of negative and positive charges. So, from the laboratory alchemist's perspective -- acid and vinegar, while they can be harsh substances that should be treated with a great deal of respect and caution, can be used with care and knowledge to accomplish a great many things.

They are not horrible, negative, forbidden, or to be avoided at all costs.

Not all parts of each Goetic seal have a symbolic alchemical meaning that I've found. There may be some random lines here and there, or random containers, that I have chalked up to creative license on the part of the artist(s) who drew the seals. I may have, in some cases, not found all of the alchemical symbols within the seal because I don't have the right alchemical symbol set, or the alchemist who wrote the book had his own. This may include the overall shape of the seal itself. I spent hours going through old alchemical symbol tables searching for matches, and every seal had matches. Some jumped out at me. Other symbols were more elusive. But sometimes there was repetition for the sake of, what I assume, was symmetry - to make the seal more aesthetically pleasing. Or to suggest the process described should be repeated. That said, I do feel that the creator(s) of the seals preferred symmetry. We cannot discount the potential explanation that actual flawed human beings had something to say about the sigils and their creation. Imagine being able to communicate a great deal of information in a single glyph. That is what the seals in the Ars Goetia are.

You'll notice that some Daemons may have symbols in the seals for other metals/elements,etc... than the ones listed for them. In instances like this, you can use the corresponding planetary, element, or metal listed, or the ones shown in the sigil. But oftentimes you'll find that these contradictions, if you want to call them that, make sense in the scope of the spirit's other attributes or purposes/uses. Adjust accordingly.

You will see two examples of each seal (for the Goetia), and in some cases, the meaning of the seal changes slightly with the different artist, though each artist does seem to understand the alchemical meanings of the seals. Whether purposeful or accidental, it gives you an idea of how Goetic seals could be modified to contain the alchemical composition you're after (or wish to communicate).

Can you look at other sigil sets, like Angels, or Daemonic sigils from other grimoires, and find alchemical symbolism? Absolutely. I've found alchemical symbolism (matching a Daemon's individual attributes) in the Grimoirium Verum set (which includes the 9 Daemonic forces of the Grand Grimoire), and have included a brief chapter for that, as well.

Does this mean I can make my own sigils using alchemical symbols? Of course. Have at it. I know the purists among you won't like this, but spirituality is subjective and if something works, I see no reason to discount it just because it's not considered canon by the wider community of practitioners. Unverified Personal Gnosis (UPG) is only UPG to the person who hasn't verified it. That means to each person new to the grimoires – the grimoires are the unverified personal gnosis to them until they work with them, and that gnosis is verified. This brings up the point that those who only do by-the-book magick are very limited in their thinking and to me, that shows a lack of personal creativity. I've always said - real magicians create. Yes, we know the rules. But we break them in meaningful ways that work, and that's an important point that distinguishes the armchair magicians with a lifestyle obsession (as a friend puts it), from the magicians actually in the magick circle getting their hands dirty. As I've heard it said many times - the limitations and one-true-ways we fight for are the limitations we saddle ourselves with.

What are Sigils?

What are sigils? Sigils are often said to be the "signatures" of the spirits or Daemons themselves. There are plenty of stories where a magician writes a pact and the Daemon itself signs the pact with its sigil. So why would human symbolism be encoded into a sigil? This is a great question and one I've pondered. If, in fact, the spirits do give us the sigils themselves, then perhaps they encoded the seals with this symbolism as a communication of their correspondences. Or perhaps the sigils are merely a synthesis of the human interpretation of all these correspondences, thus linking the practitioner to the spirit via a visual key. Something that links this world and their world in a way both spirit and practitioner can understand and use to connect with one another.

What a lot of people fail to remember is that alchemy was huge during the time Ars Goetia was written and when most of the sigils were recorded. Every last one of them, at least in Ars Goetia, and in the Grimoirium Verum, have alchemical symbols in them that are not coincidental. I've basically been doing a study of this for several years now. It's actually quite fascinating. I'm honestly surprised some people have completely ignored alchemy (the spiritual and the laboratory) as a part of their ceremonial magic. It's not a separate thing. In fact, some folks don't even notice or acknowledge that there are alchemical and astrological symbols completely relevant in almost every last sigil. Instead, they will insist that the sigil is typically considered to be a unique representation of the spirit or entity it is associated with, rather than a composite of different symbolic systems that are actually all part of the same system (alchemy).

So, ultimately, I think that most fundamental interpretations of the sigils themselves (not their usage clearly) are either superficial (i.e. animist depictions, which does have some merit since Western Alchemical emblems and drawings are rife with animal symbolism), or outright wrong (dots representing planes of existence.) I base it on the historical data and a logical conclusion based on that data. The usage of the sigils is not in question here. They are, for all intents and purposes, "signatures" of the spirits. But more importantly, they are a synthesis of information about the spirit and the processes that spirit rules over.

I'd also like to take a moment to talk about my use of the word Daemon. The word demon, often used to denote an evil or malevolent spirit, comes from the Latin Daemon and the Greek Daimon, meaning divine intelligence, or replete with wisdom. I do view these spirits as part of the divine intelligence, and therefore Daemonic. But you are welcome to just see them as spirits. I suspect the Ars Goetia spirits have been labeled "demonic" for the fact that there are a lot of harsh, poisonous, and deadly substances in the recipes, and a lot of the spiritual alchemy described by these seals and spirit descriptions isn't necessarily gentle. It's metaphoric for deep shadow work. For a certain segment of the population, their perspective of such caustic, harsh, or dramatic spiritual change may be considered evil or malevolent, even though these changes are often in the best interest of the practitioner. Sometimes things have to be destroyed in order for the practitioner to rebuild and improve.

If you're looking to do more study into alchemy, I suggest Hermes Trismegistus, *The Golden Work* or *The Golden Treatise of Hermes*. If you're curious about the symbol sets I used to interpret the seals, that's a more difficult question because there are hundreds of symbol sets. The sets I'm using come from the late 1500's to the mid 1700's. Because here's the thing, a lot of the Goetia manuscripts range from 1655-1712, so using those symbol sets makes the most sense. I've been getting a lot from *Medicinisch chymisch und alchemistisches Oraculum - 1755*, which is one of the most comprehensive listings of alchemical symbols. I think the important thing to recognize is that I'm utilizing symbology that was in use in the late 1600's when the initial prototypes of the Ars Goetia surfaced, even though people speculate the collected Lemegeton surfaced in the late 1500's. Who knows how many artists took liberties with the seals as old manuscripts were often copied by hand – and newer renditions of the seals exist everywhere. Inconsistencies certainly did happen with names of spirits in the spellings of the names, which happens when manuscripts are copied by hand. That explains why Samigina and Gamigin are the same spirit, and why there are several spellings of each Goetia spirit name. I discuss the "name game" a bit in *The Complete Book of Demonolatry* if you're interested.

That said, when you're interpreting these sigils alchemically, it really opens up the scope of the Daemon's realm of influence because it doesn't limit them to what is written in the grimoires. It expands it.

Ultimately, I do believe a practitioner needs to "connect" visually with a sigil for it to really provide that connection between themselves and the Daemonic force they're working with. Thus, this also means that each Daemonic force (i.e. Goetic spirit) may actually be code for a different alchemical principle, process, or operation both within the magician and external to the magician so it can be made manifest within us and outside of us. Some of the seals contain the makings for actual laboratory alchemical recipes. Others do not and are metaphoric for spiritual alchemical processes.

Also note that in the Ars Goetia, if it's to be taken at face value, sigils are meant to be worn as protection from the spirits (and the original text will even tell you how or where to wear it, such as on the breast), and/or to get them to obey the magician. Symbolically, wearing the seal of the spirit you're working with could mean you are becoming that spirit (process), or to get that spirit to recognize itself in you and vice versa. That's just one interpretation. Or it could just be that you need to keep the recipe at hand while attempting the experiments, so you don't harm yourself or others. Some of the seals and descriptions are outright warnings of what not to do while practicing spiritual or laboratory alchemy. Think of them as lab safety.

I hope this has given you some insight into the book overall and my headspace while writing it.

Alchemy

I think it's important when we discuss magickal work that we first define our terms so that we're all on the same page. I can't begin to tell you how many arguments in magickal communities begin over different terminology for the same thing. If we define what we mean up front, then discuss the topic, it's more likely we can start from a place of understanding and/or agreement. For example, when I think of "possession" I think of a spirit taking over a medium against that medium's will. However, some people view possession as the medium allowing the spirit (willfully) to possess the body, which is something I'd call *channeling* since the medium is in control. Believe it or not, magicians from different paradigms can often agree with one another on a good number of things. The problem is, we're usually using different terminology and genre-specific buzzwords, so we miss coming at the subject from a place of agreement. It's much easier to come to a conversation from a place of disagreement because it satisfies that magician's ego.

Here are some alchemical terms you might want to know if you don't already. (This comes from my *Daemonolater's*

Guide to Daemonic Magick and warranted repetition here.) Please note I'm sure I am missing plenty of alchemical terms here. It is by no means meant to be a complete list, but it should help if you need to look something up in a pinch.

Terminology

This terminology is included here as some of these words are used within the text, but it also gives an overview of alchemical terminology you may find useful in your studies beyond this book.

Ablation: Separating one substance from another by skimming it off the top in some manner.

Albification: Turning a substance (matter) white.

Ablution: Purification by washing with liquid, usually successively.

Amalgams: Amalgam means a mixture or blend of something. In alchemy, it means the blending of an alloy of mercury with another metal.

Assation: Reducing matter to dry ash via burning.

Calcination: Heating or burning a substance until it is broken down.

Ceration: Causing a substance to soften and become wax-like. Usually achieved by adding liquid and heating until the proper consistency is attained.

Cineration: Another word to describe heating something until it turns to ash.

Coagulation: (also Coadunation and Congelation) Turning thin liquids into solids as with curdling milk. Sometimes this involves adding something, heating, or cooling the mixture.

Coction (also Concoction): Cooking a substance at moderate heat for an extended period. Kind of like simmering (for the cooks among us), but not necessarily.

Cohobation: Removing the moisture from a substance by applying heat. In this process you'll usually find liquid re-added and the process repeated.

Colliquation: Melting together two fusible substances.

Coloration: Exactly what it says. Coloring a substance by adding dyes or colored tinctures. Sometimes it's only a surface coating, other times it's changing the entire color of a substance depending on application.

Combustion: Burning matter or substance in open air.

Comminution: Reducing the substance to powder using a mortar and pestle or forcing it through a sieve of some sort.

Composition: Mixing two substances together.

Conception: The merging of masculine and feminine aspects of substances. What's interesting is this can be taken metaphorically as indicated by substance correspondences, or literally as in male and female parts of flowers.

Conglutination (also Glutination): Turning a substance into a glue-like substance, usually by putrefaction. If you want to test this, leave spinach in butter sauce in a bowl at a window that gets sun for about a week.

Conjunction (also Copulation): Joining two opposite components. This can be utilized for polarity purposes, too. The joining of Lucifer and Lucifuge for example. Or Unsere and Eurynomous.

Contrition: Reducing something into powder via fire.

Corrosion: Allowing a substance to be eaten by a corrosive material such as something acidic or alkaline.

Cribation: Turning a substance to powder by shoving through a mesh strainer.

Crystallization: Usually formed by evaporation of liquid.

Dealbation: Changing a black substance, via alchemical process, into something very white.

Decrepitation: Splitting apart substances via heating. To test this, add a grain of salt to flame.

Deliquium: Reducing a solid to a liquid by putting it in a humid place where it can absorb water from the air. A good example of this is those canisters of moisture absorbers containing calcium chloride.

Descension: The separation of one substance from another wherein one substance sinks to the bottom of whatever it is mixed with. As opposed to *ascension* where one substance rises from another into vapor as happens with distillation.

Desiccation: Drying a substance.

Detonation: Burning a substance with the result being an explosion. Substances mixed with nitrate for example.

Digestion: Gently heating a substance to modification.

Disintegration (also Dissociation): Breaking down a substance into its many parts.

Dispoliaration: Turning dead matter into liquid.

Dissolution: Dissolving a substance in liquid.

Distillation: Separating specific components from a substance by heating, thus separating the wanted component from the substance so that it turns to vapor, which is then condensed and collected as a liquid.

Divapouration: Producing dry smoke (vapor) from a substance upon heating.

Edulceration: Removal of salts from a substance by washing.

Elaboration (also Exaltation): Purifying a substance by any variety of processes.

Elixeration: Turning a substance into an elixir.

Evaporation: Removing water from a substance via heat or general air-drying.

Exhalation: Releasing gas or air from a substance

Expression: Extracting liquids using a press.

Extraction: Macerating a substance in alcohol for purification. After extraction, the extract is then separated from the left-over residue.

Fermentation: Allowing an organic substance to rot and produce gas bubbles.

Filtration: Passing a substance through a strainer, filter, or cheesecloth to remove the pulp or matter of a substance.

Fumigation: Altering a substance by passing it through smoke. This term is often used to describe clearing a temple by filling it with smoke from incense. Of course, alchemically, the smoke should be corrosive in some way.

Fusion: Mixing two powders or converting a substance into a new form via exposure to high heat.

Gradation: Gradually purifying a substance by performing the purification process in stages.

Granulation: Turning a substance to powder or grain by grinding, pounding, heating with rapid cooling etc…

Grinding: Using a mortar and pestle to reduce material to a powder.

Humectation: Allowing a substance to absorb moisture by placing it in a humid environment.

Imbibition: The process of continually adding gradual substance to another substance.

Impastation: When a substance that has been through putrefaction and becomes black, thick and congealed.

Impregnation: Taking a male substance and a female substance, infusing them via copulation and creating a new substance.

Inceration: Adding water to give a substance the consistency of soft wax.

Incineration: Using fire to turn a substance to ash.

Incorporation: Mixing together different substances until they become one body.

Ingression: Combining two substances in a way that they cannot be separated later.

Inhumation: To bury a substance in earth.

Liquefaction: Melting or dissolving a solid substance into liquid.

Maturation: A degree of perfection of the work.

Melting: Turning metal or other substances to liquid via heating.

Mortification: Allowing the substance to go through a death (usually via putrefaction), seemingly destroyed but later revived.

Multiplication: Multiplying the power of a substance.

Projection: Using a tincture or ferment on a substance in order to transform the substance.

Pulverization: Beating a substance into smaller fragments using a hammer or mallet.

Putrefaction: Letting a substance rot through use of a gentle moist heat, causing the substance to become black.

Quinta Essentia: An elevated form of a substance. Making of a quintessence.

Rarefaction: Making a substance thin, airy, and subtle.

Rectification: Purification of a substance by repeated distillation (i.e. Reiteration).

Reiteration: The repeated distillation of a substance.

Resolution: A process similar to coagulation where substances are mixed together and become separated when placed in a solution.

Restinction: Perfecting a substance at white heat by quenching it in an exalted liquid.

Reverberation: Igniting a substance at high temperature as within a furnace. Calcination via high temperatures.

Revivification: Reactivating mortified matter.

Rubification: Making matter go from white to red via alchemical process.

Segregation: Separating a substance into all of its parts. The separation of a composite substance into its parts.

Separation: Taking two opposite components together and removing one from the other. This process is often alternated with conjunction.

Stratification: A process in which a substance is reduced to lathers of its various properties in the flask. The heavier parts of the substance will sink while subsequent lighter materials will float to different lathers in the flask.

Sublimation: Heating matter to where it gives off vapor, which then condenses in the cooler upper part of the vessel without going through a liquid phase.

Subtilation: Separating a subtle part of a substance from the bulk of it. For example, separating essential oil from a plant leaf.

Transudation: Sweating the essence out of a substance in drops during a descending distillation.

Trituration: Reducing a substance to powder by applying heat.

Vitrification: Turning a substance into glass by using high heat and sometimes adding lime.

Common Alchemical Symbolism

Obviously, of the most common alchemical symbols found in the emblems of the Ars Goetia is the circle. Symbolically it represents unity and wholeness and is often used to represent the divine or spiritual realm. In some schools of thought, the sigil should be enclosed in a circle to depict focus on a particular force, or without a circle to symbolize the connection to the whole. Other people believe the exact opposite of this - that encircled, a sigil represents the energy force being part of the whole while the lack of the circle suggests focus on the spirit's energy. In the context of alchemy, the latter seems more appropriate, but you can work with the sigils circled or not circled according to your preference.

Another common symbol you'll find within alchemy is the triangle, which represents balance and harmony. The triangle is often used to represent the three elements of alchemy: sulfur, mercury, and salt. That said, triangles are used to represent the elements as well. The triangle pointing upward is for fire. The triangle with the point down symbolizes water. A line crossing the first third of an upward pointing triangle is used for air, while flipped upside down, it's used to represent earth. That line, perhaps, represents the sky (air) and the ground (earth).

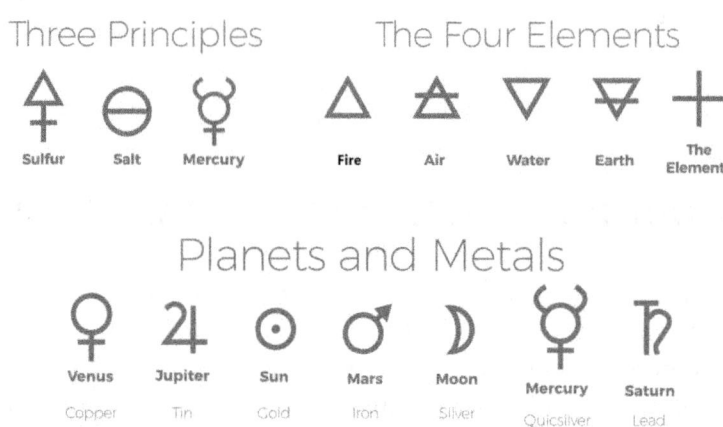

Some other common symbols are the equal-armed cross, which represents the four elements of earth, air, fire, and water; the pentagram, which represents the five elements of earth, air, fire, water, and spirit; and the hexagram, which represents the six elements of earth, air, fire, water, spirit, and soul. Inverse pentagrams suggest man in control of the elements, while the right side up pentagram represents the elements of creation or the elements in relation to the spirit.

Animals in Alchemy and Their Meanings

In addition to the common alchemical symbols, animal imagery played an important role in alchemy. You'll find that some sigils and some descriptions of the spirits often incorporate images of animals such as snakes, lions, and eagles or the sigil itself has a shape that looks very animal like. My favorite example of this is the sigil for Amy, which reminds me of a cat. Cats symbolize transformation and hidden knowledge. And, not surprisingly, the spirit, Amy, does bestow hidden knowledge upon the magician whether it's teaching astrology, giving the magician images via divination, or helping the magician find elusive "treasure" (often a code-word for hidden knowledge or wisdom worth its weight in gold) - the alchemical cat symbology works. Animal depictions are often used to represent various aspects of alchemical transformation. For example, the lion (Marbas comes to mind) represents strength and courage as well as individual ascension and gold, whereas snakes are associated with rebirth and regeneration, also wisdom, and the eagle represents the completion of the Magnum Opus (or great work) or the ascension of the soul.

In illuminated alchemical manuscripts, you'll see this animal symbolism in action as well. A quick glance at the images in the *Splendor Solis*, for example, and you'll be greeted with birds of all types and colorful peacocks. Some of the animals I have listed do not actually have a traditional western alchemical significance, but I included the symbolism of the animal regardless for the edification of those who might be curious. Plus, you will find certain animals, like the Camel, being associated with spirits like Paimon, even though camels don't really hold any specific significance in western alchemy overall, not that I could find anyway. Instead, the camel symbolism may have come into play in earlier Arabic alchemical texts, suggesting that the Ars Goetia was, indeed, drawing on older Arabic manuscripts in some way.

ALLIGATORS/CROCODILES – In the Ars Goetia, you'll sometimes find spirits riding upon crocodiles. While I could not find any information linking alligators or crocodiles to western alchemy overall, they do have a spiritual meaning. We have to remember that most pre-Judeo-Christian religions were not only pagan, but also animists. The Egyptian goddess, Sobek, the goddess of the Nile, for example, who ruled over fertility (crops need water to grow), protection, and power, was depicted as a crocodile. Alligators and crocodiles, being some of the largest reptiles that can live on both land and water, were seen as special messengers of the gods. Some cultures believed that crocodiles or alligators appeared to people whenever a large change was about to occur in their lives. They have been associated with protection, as stated above, as well as cleansing and purification.

BATS – Bats are another creature that aren't necessarily associated with western alchemy, but have been associated with Daemonic spirits such as Lilith. They are often symbols of adaptation, determination, strength, and perseverance. Some cultures even see them as symbolic of the journey of the soul transcending from the darkness to the light.

BEARS – In the western alchemical tradition, bears often symbolize transformation. Bears are associated with the first chakra, which represents the physical body and the needs of the physical body. In other cultures, they symbolize bravery, strength, and protection.

BEETLES/BUGS – In this section, I'll not only go through Beetles, but other insects as well. Please note that spiders have their own section. While beetles do not usually appear in western alchemical manuscripts, they are associated with strength and power as well as persistence.

They represent a resilience in transformation and change through that strength. In some cultures, beetles are viewed as an auspicious omen that brings opportunity, abundance, and wealth.

Scarab – While not necessarily an alchemical symbol, the scarab was an important symbol in ancient Egypt. The scarab is a dung beetle (Scarabaeus sacer), which lays its eggs in dung balls fashioned through rolling. The beetle was associated with the divine manifestation of the early morning sun, Khepri. The scarab was also associated with the concept of rebirth and regeneration. Often used in amulets and jewelry, the scarab was believed to have protective powers.

Bugs (General) – Bugs in general are often associated with transformations, metamorphosis, and change. In many different cultures, different bugs are seen as symbolic of good luck and prosperity overall, or protection. I suppose it depends on the type of bug and the culture we're looking at.

Butterflies/Moths - In traditional western alchemy, butterflies and moths are not commonly used as symbols. However, in modern alchemy, people have associated butterflies as representative of alchemical Mercury - a psychic substance that acts as an intermediary, forming a bridge between the conscious and the unconscious. They represent internal illumination and manifestation of the self, likely due to the process of the metamorphosis that butterflies go through. That said, moths are not commonly associated with alchemy either, but in many cultures, they are often seen as symbols of transformation, change, and rebirth, again due to their metamorphic life cycle.

Dragonflies - While not used in alchemical symbolism,

Dragonflies have been part of various cultural beliefs over the centuries. In some modern alchemical contexts, the dragonfly is associated with the concept of transmutation, the process of turning base metals into gold, or the pursuit of spiritual transformation.

BIRDS - (See Eagles for birds of prey) Birds are common symbols in alchemy, representing the different aspects of the alchemical process and the spiritual transformation of the alchemist. Birds, as creatures of the air element, mediate between the earthly realm and the heavenly world, and reflect the inner experiences of personal transformation. Some modern alchemical schools of thought call this soul alchemy.

Some of the most important birds in alchemy represent the five stages of the alchemical work:

1. **Crows** – blackening, putrefaction, the first stage of the alchemical work, where the impure matter is decomposed and purified. (See Crows later in this chapter as they have their own section.)

2. **Swans** – whitening, washing, the second stage of the alchemical work, where the purified matter is cleansed and refined.

3. **Peacocks** – multicolored, iridescence, the third stage of the alchemical work, where the refined matter shows various colors and patterns, indicating the presence of the hidden essence. (See Peacocks later in this chapter.)

4. **Pelican** – represents self-sacrifice and rebirth, the fourth stage of alchemical work, where the essence is extracted and nourished by the alchemist, who sacrifices his own blood or life force.

5. **Phoenix** – while a purely fictional bird, it represents completion and resurrection, the fifth and final stage of the alchemical work, where the essence is. (See Phoenix)

BUFFALO – the buffalo has been a symbol of power, strength, and abundance in many cultures. In animal alchemy, the buffalo is associated with the element of earth and represents the physical body and its needs. It is also associated with the color brown, which symbolizes stability and grounding. Some believe the buffalo represents the power of the unconscious mind and the ability to manifest one's desires.

CATS - (See also Lions) Cats represent mystery and hidden knowledge. They imbue the energy of transformation. They are the guardians of that which is sacred. This is probably one of many reasons why cats and witches became intertwined throughout history. In alchemical manuscripts, they often suggest the complexity of an alchemical operation as they're often found alongside other alchemical symbolism depicting more elaborate alchemical formulas. Cats also represent duality - the light and the darkness, the hidden and the revealed. They are thought to be able to walk between the mundane and spirit worlds, which is why they often make good familiars.

CAMEL – Camels (or dromedaries) are not commonly used as western alchemical symbols, except in instances where there may have been an Arabic alchemy influence. In spiritualism, the camel is believed to be a powerful spirit animal that represents safety, endurance, persistence, adaptation, travel, resilience, and survival. According to a friend, the camel may have played an important role in 7th century Arabic alchemy. The camel survived in the extreme heat of the desert and may have symbolized *enduring* *through fire*. It's that same alchemical concept of being purified or tempered by fire. If the Ars Goetia is western alchemy, then you may wonder why spirits like Paimon ride upon camels if is there no western alchemical significance. It is this author's opinion that the recipe or process Paimon represents likely came from an Arabic alchemical source. We can also rationalize that oftentimes, large mammals in western alchemy, represented the earth, matter, and the physical body, so it's very possible the dromedaries of the Ars Goetia could hold that symbolism as well. But again, it is possible that some of these recipes were, in fact, copied from Arabic alchemical texts, as there was once a rich Arabic alchemical tradition. Though it was clearly translated and rewritten in western alchemical medieval symbolism, perhaps keeping the camel imagery to add further mystery to the manuscript.

CHICKENS (includes pullets) The chicken does have some significance in alchemy, as it is one of the animals associated with mercury. Mercury, also known as quicksilver, is a symbol of fluidity, transformation, and communication. Quicksilver is often depicted as a winged serpent, but sometimes also as a rooster, a raven, or a dragon. In some cultures, the rooster or chicken represents the rising of the sun, the dawn of a new day, and the awakening of the spirit. In western alchemy, the chicken is also a symbol of the philosopher's stone, the elusive substance that can turn base metals into gold and grant immortality. The philosopher's stone is sometimes called the "red lion" or the "golden cock" and is said to hatch from an egg after a long and complex process of purification and refinement. For those of you curious about *The Black Pullet* —a grimoire of talismans, a pullet is a young female chicken that is less than three years old and has not yet started laying eggs. See the chapter on alchemical colors for the significance of the color black in alchemy.

COWS - While not often used as a symbol in alchemy, cows are almost universally associated with life's continuance, motherhood, and the mother goddesses. Among Hindu communities, the cow is sacred. This is why Hindus do not eat beef and treat their cows with great respect. Deities with cow associations like the Egyptian goddess, Nut, act like a nursemaid to humankind, particularly mothers and children. Images of Nut show her as a giant cow that embodies the heavens, and her titles include "she who bore the Gods" and "she who protects."

Bulls – Bulls are often symbolic of the element earth. In alchemy, the bull is also a symbol of the first stage of the alchemical work. This stage involves the decomposition or purification of the raw material by fire. The primal matter that must be destroyed and dissolved before it can transform into something higher.

CRABS - Crabs are often associated with adaptation, strength, determination, and perseverance. They are also seen as a symbol of the soul, representing the journey of the soul from darkness to light. In western alchemy, crabs are not commonly used as symbols.

CROWS - The crow is a symbol that has been used in alchemy to represent various concepts. According to Carl Jung, the crow is associated with the beginning of the great work. The beginning of this work includes the initial stages of the alchemist's encounter with his inner workings by withdrawing from the outer world and gazing inward (via meditation) into the dark shadow-self. Crows are also associated with metamorphosis, transformation, and passage, which are strongly symbolized by all birds in the Corvidae family, which includes both crows and ravens.

DEER (also Stags) - Deer are associated with the alchemical Mercury, acting as an intermediary, forming the bridge between the conscious and the unconscious. Kind of like in yoga when they say the breath is the bridge between the body and mind. It is a similar concept. Deer have also been associated with tenderness tempered with strength. Tough love comes to mind – nudging one in the right direction while also being understanding and nurturing.

DOGS - Dogs are a common symbol in alchemy, and their meaning can vary depending on the context. I suppose a lot of things vary based on context, but some symbols more than others. While culturally dogs are often associated with friendship, loyalty, and protection, in a spiritual context they are symbolic of the soul. In some cases, the journey of the soul from darkness to light. In other cases, dogs are used to represent the philosopher's stone.

DOVES - In alchemy, doves are another symbol often associated with the soul, and representing the journey of the soul from darkness to light. They are associated with the concept of transformation and change, symbolizing potential growth and change within oneself.

EAGLES (and Hawks and Falcons) - In alchemy, overall, the eagle represents the completion of the Magnum Opus (Great Work) and the ascension of the mind and spirit. A powerful alchemical symbol, it can also represent different aspects of the alchemical process and the spiritual transformation of the alchemist. There are three meanings:

First, the eagle represents the air element, which is associated with intellect, communication, and creativity. It can also symbolize the power of vision, intuition, and spiritual awareness – perspective even. In some cultures, the eagle is viewed as a messenger from the spirit realm to bring guidance to all who seek it.

Second, the eagle is sometimes used as a symbol of purified sulfur, which is one of the three essential substances in alchemy, along with mercury and salt. Sulfur represents the active, masculine, and fiery principle, which is necessary for the generation of life and the transformation of matter.

Third, the eagle can symbolize the stage of sublimation, which is one of the steps in the alchemical process of turning base metals into gold. Sublimation is the process of heating a solid substance until it becomes a gas, and then cooling it down until it becomes a solid again, but with a higher purity and quality. The eagle is often seen as a symbol of the alchemist himself, who undergoes a spiritual transformation and attains a higher state of being.

Hawks and Falcons: In alchemy, hawks and falcons have different meanings and symbolism, depending on the context and the source. Much like the eagle, hawks also represent the element of air, which is associated with intellect, communication, and creativity. Hawks also symbolize the power of vision, intuition, and spiritual awareness. They, too, are often seen as messengers from the spirit realm, bringing guidance and insight to those who seek it. Hawks may also represent determination, focus, leadership, and courage.

Falcons, on the other hand, represent the element of fire, which is associated with energy, passion, and transformation. In some cultures, falcons also symbolize the power of speed, accuracy, and skill. They are often seen as hunters, warriors, and protectors, who pursue their goals with fierce determination and confidence. Falcons may also represent nobility, vigilance, and wisdom.

In some alchemical texts, eagles, hawks and falcons are used as symbols of the stages of the alchemical process. For example, in the *Rosarium Philosophorum*, a medieval alchemical manuscript, there is an illustration of a hawk and a falcon fighting each other, which represents the stage of dissolution, where the opposing forces of nature are separated and purified. The hawk represents the volatile principle of mercury, while the falcon represents the fixed principle of sulfur.

Another example is in the *Splendor Solis*, a 16th-century alchemical manuscript, where there is an illustration of a falcon devouring a crow, which represents the stage of calcination, where the impure matter is burned away, and the essence is revealed. The falcon represents the alchemical fire, while the crow represents the blackness of the prima materia, or the raw material of the alchemical work.

FISH - Fish are another common symbol in alchemy, and again, their meaning can vary depending on the context. Fish, too, have been associated with the alchemical Mercury. Associated with the concept of transmutation, fish represent the pursuit of spiritual transformation. In addition, fish are often associated with the unconscious, representing the hidden depths of the psyche and the journey of the soul. Fish are also associated with the concept of the "prima materia."

FOXES – In alchemy, the fox is, perhaps, one of the most notable as people viewed the fox as the cultivators of the Elixir of Life. Alchemists of the past allegedly believed that the fox could transform itself (as an animal totem, of course) into human form. Apparently, this would happen mostly at night so they could visit the sick and the elderly. In doing this, the foxes would provide these people with a mysterious elixir to promote their health and to prolong their lives. While likely a story told for the benefit of comfort, the story is a metaphor for transformative inner healing. The fox is a solar animal attached to the symbol of fire and all its meanings.

FROGS/TOADS - Frogs and toads have been associated with various symbolic meanings in alchemy including transformation and change within the self. It's no wonder fairy tales turned princes into frogs who could only be transformed by the kiss of a beautiful princess. In Western alchemy, one can find depictions of the symbolic toad tethered to the eagle to illustrate how the volatile elements of the spirit must be grounded in reality.

GOATS - Goats are a symbol of power, independence, and ambition in many cultures. In alchemy, goats are often associated with the four elements: Earth, Fire, Air, and Water. They are also seen as a symbol of the soul and its ascension from the darkness to the light. Goats have also been associated with fertility, virility, and desire, symbolizing creative energy and the ability to tap into our imaginations and create. Which is why it makes sense that The Baphomet is depicted as a goat and in itself, has become a symbol of the balance and unity.

The Baphomet: Associated with the "Sabbatic Goat" image drawn by Éliphas Lévi, Baphomet combines numerous binary elements representing an equilibrium of opposites. It is half-human and half-goat, male and female, good and evil, comprised of all the elements of creation etc. Lévi's intention was to symbolize balance.

Esoterically, Baphomet represents the alchemical Great Work and embodies the concept of *As Above, So Below*. On its arms are written *coagula* and *solve*. The phrase "Solve et coagula" is a principle that underlies alchemy. It means to dissolve materials to their constituents and reassemble them into something else. The phrase is often associated with the process of eternal alchemical rebirth, where "solve" means breaking down of elements. This process is said to reveal the energy that animates these elements. Or, with mental alchemy, resolving that which is unresolved – like bad feelings, or feelings of inadequacy. The word "coagula" means to join together and take apart. In the context of Lévi's work, these two terms represent the dualistic power of magick, accessible to the initiate.

HORSES - (and Unicorns) Horses are a symbol of power, freedom, and endurance in many cultures. In alchemy, like many large mammals, horses are often associated with the four elements: Earth, Fire, Air, and Water

Unicorns - (as with the spirit Amdusias) In the *Chemical Wedding of Christian Rosencreutz*, a snow-white unicorn appears and makes his obeisance before a lion. Both the lion and unicorn are symbols of Mercurius - a transformative substance which allows the process of transmutation to occur. The unicorn is also associated with the beginning of the great work and indicates the initial stages of the alchemist's encounter with his shadow self.

IBIS - The Ibis has been featured in alchemical texts as representative of the moon and all the planetary powers it possesses, including intuition, wisdom, insight, the ebb and flow of the tides, and the cyclic nature of the moon's phases, as well as the passage of time. In the past, people placed a great amount of importance on the moon as a way to ensure successful transmutation. The Egyptian god Thoth is depicted with the head of an Ibis. The god of writing, wisdom, and magick, he was also a moon god and is often associated with Hermes Trismegistus.

LIONS - (see below for other big cats) Alchemically, the lion is a solar creature that represents gold (the ultimate metal) and the sun. It represents individual ascension and enlightenment. The alchemists viewed lions as the protectors of alchemical secrets. In many cultures they represent strength, courage, and virility. People also viewed them as the keepers and guardians of the underworld.

Other Large Cats:
Leopards are a symbol of power, strength, and confidence in many cultures. In alchemy, the leopard is associated with the element of fire and represents the power of transformation and regeneration. It is also considered a symbol of the unconscious mind and its ability to manifest one's desires.

Cheetahs - In alchemy, the cheetah is not a commonly used symbol. However, in spiritualism, the cheetah represents courage, determination, and uniqueness.

Panthers are also not commonly used as alchemical symbols, and have a similar symbolism to cheetahs.

Tigers have been a symbol of power, strength, courage, and control in various cultures. In alchemy though, tigers are not commonly used as symbols.

LIZARDS -While not generally used in alchemical symbolism, lizards are often associated with adaptation, strength, determination, and perseverance.

MYTHOLOGICAL BEASTS

Fauns - Half human, half goat (part deer) - There are no alchemical meanings for fauns. A faun is a half-human and half-goat mythological creature that appears in Greek and Roman mythology. Originally, fauns of Roman mythology were ghosts (genii) of wild places. They were symbols of peace and fertility. Fauns were often depicted as two-footed creatures with the horns, legs, and tail of a deer and the head, torso, and arms of a human; they are often depicted with pointed ears. The horned god of many mythologies comes to mind.

Griffins - The griffin combines features of a lion and an eagle. In alchemy, the griffin symbolizes the union of the elements of fire and air, as well as the power of transformation and transmutation. The griffin also represents the alchemical process of sublimation, which is the conversion of a solid substance into a gas or vapor. Some alchemists also associated the griffin with the philosopher's stone. The philosopher's stone, allegedly, could turn base metals into gold and grant immortality.

Centaurs - half human, half horse -- centaurs are creatures from Greek mythology with the upper body of a human and the lower body and legs of a horse. They were said to live in the mountains of Thessaly and were considered, in many Greek myths, to be as wild as untamed horses. In alchemy, centaurs are often associated with the union of opposites – like the union of the conscious and unconscious mind. The human half of the centaur represents the conscious mind, while the horse half represents the unconscious mind.

Dragons - The dragon is a symbol of the prime matter, the raw material from which all things are created. It represents chaos before order and is the first stage of alchemy – the blackening or nigredo, where the prime matter is putrefied and dissolved. It is also representative of sulfur – an active fiery principle that drives alchemical transformation. If **wingless**, the dragon may symbolize the Ouroboros, the unity of opposites and the cyclic nature of life and time and the renewal of all things. The **two-headed dragon** represents the volatile union of sulfur and mercury, which must be harmonized with the alchemical process to maintain balance.

Mermaids: Mermaids represent the soul and the connection of the soul with emotion. This mythological creature is the feminine divine and represents external transformations and internal enlightenment. Mermaids possess dual personalities: one side benevolent, the other potentially malevolent. This mirrors the alchemical concept of opposing forces—solve et coagula (dissolve and coagulate).

Unicorns (see under Horses)

OSTRICH - The ostrich also has a small, but important role in alchemy. Due to legends that state the ostrich's stomach is capable of digesting just about anything, it prompted alchemists to associate the bird with various types of acids. In alchemy, these acids were used in the processes of transforming ordinary gold and silver into their grand philosophic counterparts.

OWLS - Owls are associated with the ouroboros. One possible connection between them is that they both represent wisdom and the cyclical nature of life. The owl is often associated with wisdom, knowledge, and insight in many cultures. The owl, also being a nocturnal creature, symbolizes the ability to see through the darkness and uncover hidden truths. The ouroboros is a serpent or dragon that eats its own tail, forming a circle. It is an ancient symbol that originated in Egypt and was later adopted by the Greeks, Gnostics, alchemists, and other traditions. The ouroboros symbolizes the eternal cycle of life, death, and rebirth, as well as the unity of all things, material and spiritual. Both the owl and the ouroboros can be seen as symbols of wisdom, as they imply a deep understanding of the mysteries of existence and the natural order of things. They also both reflect the cyclical nature of life, as the owl is linked to the phases of the moon and the seasons, and the ouroboros is linked to the solar year and the cosmic cycle. You'll find several Goetic spirits associated with owls, one of the most popular being Stolas.

PEACOCK - The peacock is a symbol of great glory, immortality, and incorruptibility. Ancient people also saw the peacock as a symbol of integrity. In western alchemy, the peacock's tail symbolizes a stage in the alchemical process where the solution goes through a transformation of colors. It also symbolizes the ennoble aspect of matter.

PHOENIX - The phoenix, the bird that sacrifices itself in fire only to be reborn in the ashes, represents death and rebirth. It symbolizes the purifying and transforming nature of fire and sulfur. It can also symbolize resurrection.

RABBITS/HARES - Rabbits are another common symbol in alchemy, representing different aspects of the alchemical process and the spiritual transformation of the alchemist. They are creatures of the earth element, and are associated with fertility, longevity, and rebirth. They also have paradoxical qualities, such as being timid and courageous, innocent and cunning, chaste and prolific.

Some of the meanings of rabbit colors in alchemy include:

White Rabbit – a symbol of purified salt, which is one of the three essential substances in alchemy, along with sulfur and mercury. Salt represents the passive, feminine, and earthy principle, which is necessary for the clarity and manifestation of alchemical work. The white rabbit also symbolizes the power of innocence, curiosity, and purity, as it leads the alchemist into the unknown.

Black Rabbit – a symbol of the blackening, which is the first stage of the alchemical work, where the impure matter is decomposed and purified. The black rabbit also symbolizes the power of death, decay, and transformation, as it burrows into the dark earth and emerges with new life.

RATS/MICE - Rats and mice are often associated with adaptation, strength, determination, and perseverance. In western alchemy, rats and mice are not commonly used as symbols.

RAVENS - Black ravens were often taboo in ancient alchemy as they were considered the birds with the transformative powers of death and decay. People also noted them for their ability to decompose everything in their paths due to the fact that they are adaptable scavengers. Although somewhat dark and unsavory, decomposition is a necessary process for the body and soul to join. Although ravens were often viewed as an omen of death, people called upon them in alchemy during complicated operations and transmutations. Amon and Andras come to mind as raven-headed spirits in Ars Goetia.

SCORPIONS - Scorpions are often associated with adaptation, strength, determination, and perseverance much like insects. In western alchemy, they are not commonly used as symbols.

SNAKES (and OROBAS or UROBOROS) - The snake itself has been a symbol of wisdom and knowledge for most of recorded history. The snake in the Garden of Eden in Judeo-Christian mythology represented Satan as the bringer of knowledge by tempting Eve to eat the apple that revealed the true nature of the world to her. As we move forward, we find the Uroboros, a circular serpent, representing the cyclical nature of the alchemical work. This serpent is depicted swallowing its tail. It is representative of the eternal processes and cycles, like those found in alchemy. Like the phoenix, people considered this creature a symbol of the concept of rebirth and regeneration. The Uroboros was alchemy's most powerful symbol for the fundamental belief that "one is all" and "the all is one." Ars Goetia includes a lot of **Vipers** as well. **Vipers** can represent multiple things, including protection, transformation and rebirth, duality and balance, as well as wisdom and healing.

SPIDERS – Spiders, while not generally found in western alchemical manuscripts, are the perfect symbol for dualism in the physical realm. They represent the power of creativity and manifestations balanced by destruction.

WOLVES – In alchemy, the wolf is a symbol of antimony, a metal used in alchemy to purify gold. The wolf also represents the wild spirit or animalistic nature of man (and all of physical nature), which needed to be tamed or sacrificed as part of the alchemical process. The wolf is often depicted devouring the lion, a symbol of gold, and then being burned to ash, from which new, purer gold would emerge. The wolf is also a metaphor for the death and rebirth of the both the spirit and matter.

In conclusion of this list, as you're reading the grimoires, consider the alchemical animal symbolism when animals are brought up in the context of spirit descriptions or if a sigil reminds you of a particular animal. You may also find this list helpful while perusing reprints of illuminated alchemical manuscripts or alchemical artwork from the sixteenth and seventeenth centuries.

Colors and Alchemy

Colors were also important in alchemical emblems and medieval manuscripts. You'll also notice their mention in grimoires, as they indicate different stages of the alchemical work, as well as different qualities and properties of matter. You'll find all the spirits of the Ars Goetia have a color associated with them.

Here is a list of some colors and their meanings in alchemy:

Black: Black is the color of the first stage of the alchemical work, called nigredo or blackening. It represented the death and decay of matter, the dissolution of the old, and the purification of the impure. It was also associated with the element of earth, the planet Saturn, and the metal lead. The single knight, Furcas, in Ars Goetia sports the color black.

Blue: According to Carl Jung, a psychologist who studied alchemy and its symbols, blue represents a cool and calming state, a spiritual vessel, and the unconscious. In some Eastern traditions, blue is the color of the sky and the heavens, and the color of blackness and the underworld. In ancient Egypt, the god Osiris, who ruled over the dead, was often depicted in black or blue. Blue is also related to the element of water, which symbolizes the fluidity, transformation, and communication of mercury, one of the main alchemical substances. All of the princes of the Ars Goetia are associated with the color blue.

Brown: The color brown is not very common in alchemy, but it has some connections to the element of earth and the Root Chakra. Earth represents the physical/material world and boasts the qualities of cold and dryness.

Gold: The color gold in alchemy symbolizes the perfection of all matter on any level, including the mind, spirit, and soul. It represents the creation of the philosopher's stone, which can turn base metals into gold and grant immortality. Gold is associated with the sun, the element of fire, and its qualities are hot and dry.

Green: Green is the color of the intermediate stage between black and white, called viriditas or greenness. It represents the vitality and growth of matter, the emergence of the seed, and the potential for transformation. It is associated with the element of water, the planet Venus, and the metal copper. Copper turns green during oxidation – a chemical reaction to its exposure to air and water. All of Ars Goetia's dukes have the correspondence color green.

Orange: The color orange is uncommon in the greater realm of alchemy, but it has some connections to the element of fire and the Sacral Chakra. It is a combination of red and yellow, suggesting a balance between fire and air and could symbolize the process of sublimation. All the presidents of Ars Goetia are associated with orange.

Purple: (also Violet) The color purple is also not considered overly significant in alchemy, but it does connect to the element of fire. Because purple is a combination of red and blue, it can be seen as a balance between fire and water, or between passion and calmness. It can symbolize the transformation of matter into something higher and more refined, or the union of opposites into a harmonious whole. All the marquis of Ars Goetia are associated with the color violet.

Red: Red is the color of the third and final stage of the alchemical work, called rubedo or reddening. It represents the completion and perfection of matter, the union of opposites, and the creation of the philosopher's stone, the ultimate goal of alchemy. It is associated with the element of fire, the planet (celestial body) Sol (the sun), and the metal gold. The earls of Ars Goetia are associated with the color red.

Silver: The color silver in alchemy symbolizes the feminine principle, the moon, and the unconscious. It is one of the three base metals that alchemists used as the raw material for their work, along with gold and mercury. Silver is associated with purity, intuition, reflection, and wisdom. It is also related to the process of argyropeia, which means turning a base metal into silver.

White: White is the color of the second stage of the alchemical work, called albedo or whitening. It represents the washing and cleansing of matter, the separation of the pure from the impure, and the emergence of a new substance. It is associated with the element of air, the moon, and the metal silver.

Yellow: Yellow is the color of the transition stage between white and red, called citrinitas or yellowing. It represents the maturation and ripening of matter, the illumination of the mind, and the preparation for the final stage. It is associated with the element of air, the planet Mercury, and the metal mercury. All Kings in the Ars Goetia have the color yellow.

As a quick recap for colors in the Ars Goetia:

Kings: Yellow
Dukes: Green
Princes: Blue
Marquis: Violet
Presidents: Orange
Earls: Red
Knights: Black

Notice that some spirits have multiple offices, but it's the first office that I've given the color for. That said, do consider reading the color for the second office in conjunction with the first. You'll also notice that the planetary/celestial correspondence will match to that color correspondence as each celestial correspondence has a color as well. For example – Venus – copper – and green often go together. Or Jupiter, blue, and tin.

Also remain cognizant of the elements and their overall meanings. Some keywords to keep in mind for elements might include:

Earth – Stability, fertility, foundation, manifestation.

Air – Communication, intelligence, thinking, focus, clarity.

Fire – Active, passion, inspiration, creativity, forward moving, transformation, purification.

Water – Emotion, intuition, wisdom, cleansing, adaptability.

Feel free to add additional keywords to this list to help you remember the concepts behind each element.

For additional correspondences like planetary (celestial) and elemental - see *The Daemonolater's Book of Foundational Correspondences.* You'll find that many foundational correspondences tend to run through most western magickal traditions from ceremonial magick and alchemy, to Wicca, modern witchcraft, and even folk magick. While some correspondences shift or vary slightly from tradition to tradition, knowing that they exist can make learning any magickal system a bit easier.

A Key of Alchemical Symbols

See the additional reading list at the back of this book for all the books of symbols you should have at your disposal if you wish to explore the sigils of the Goetia (and other grimoires) at your own leisure. You may very well see something I've missed, or something completely different. I highly recommend *Alchemical Symbols 4th Edition* by Philip Wheeler along with Adam McLean's *Alchemical Symbols* which does a much better job of laying out the symbols from the *Medicinisch Chymisch und Alchemistisches Oraculum*.

SYMBOL SET IMAGES FROM "MEDICINISCH CHYMISCH UND ALCHEMISTISCHES ORACULUM" IN PHYSICAL COPIES OF THE BOOK ONLY FOR QUICK REFERENCE. I highly recommend you have the above two books handy while perusing this book because these images aren't nearly as clear as they are in the above mentioned texts.

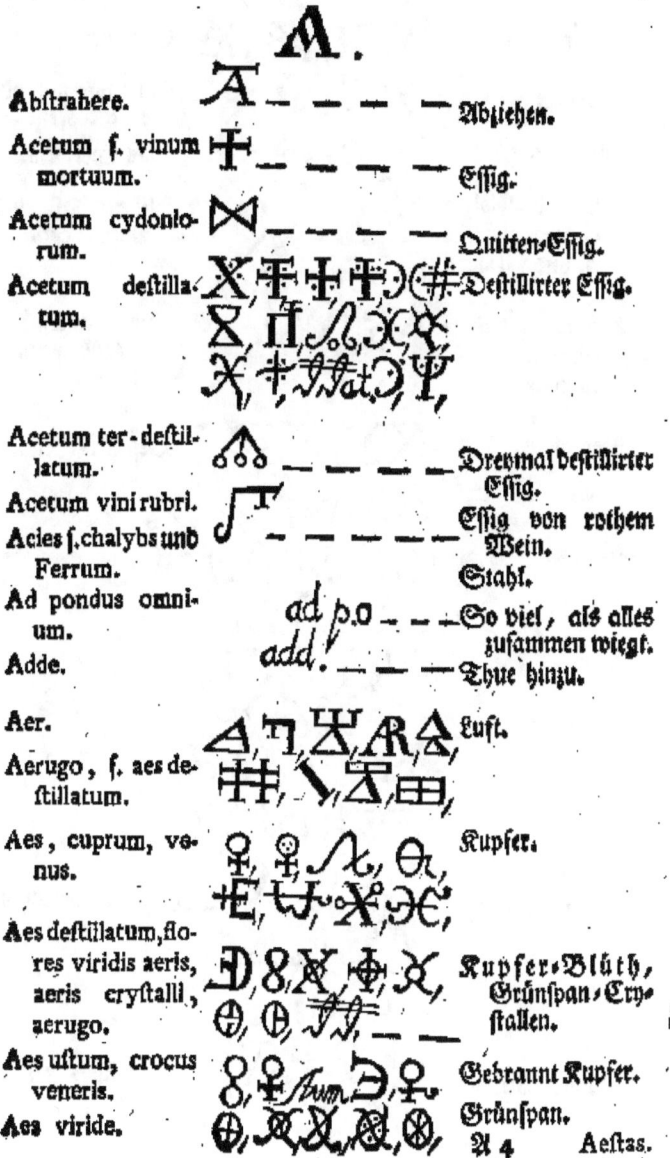

Abstrahere.	Abziehen.
Acetum f. vinum mortuum.	Essig.
Acetum cydoniorum.	Quitten-Essig.
Acetum destillatum.	Destillirter Essig.
Acetum ter-destillatum.	Dreymal destillirter Essig.
Acetum vini rubri.	Essig von rothem Wein.
Acies f. chalybs und Ferrum.	Stahl.
Ad pondus omnium.	So viel, als alles zusammen wiegt.
Adde.	Thue hinzu.
Aer.	Luft.
Aerugo, f. aes destillatum.	
Aes, cuprum, venus.	Kupfer.
Aes destillatum, flores viridis aeris, aeris crystalli, aerugo.	Kupfer-Blüth, Grünspan-Crystallen.
Aes ustum, crocus veneris.	Gebrannt Kupfer.
Aes viride.	Grünspan.

Aestas.

Aestas.	⚒, ♓, ⚹, ⚹	Sommer.
Ahenum.	⚴, ⊖, ⊙	Ein kupferner oder eiserner Keſſel.
Albumen.	♂, ♌, ⊙	Das Eyerweiß.
Alcali, alkali ſal, ſ. Cineres clavellati, und Sal alcali.	⚴, 8, ⌧, ℧, ℧	Aſchen-Salz, ſiehe alumen catinum.
Alcohol vini, Spiritus vini rectificatiſſimus.	ᵛℛ, ᵛℳ. − −	Der allerſtärkſte Brandewein.
Alembicus.	✕, ✕, ⋈, ℨ, ⋊, ℨ, ⅃, ⌐	Deſtillir-Helm.
Alumen.	⊙ 8, ∑, ♑, ⋂, ∨, ⎕, ⚛, ⊥, Ψ, ♓, ♌, ⊕, ∪, ♄, Ψ, ⌣, ⬜, ô, ⁊, π, ⱶ, â, ∞, ♌	Alaun.
Alumen calcinatum, uſtum.	ℛ, ⌇, ∧, ⏄, ⎾, ⚒, ⚔, ⚒, ⊕	Gebrannter Alaun.
Alumen çatinum.	⚭, ♃, ⚴, ⱶ, ⎋	Potaſche, Weidaſche. Alu-

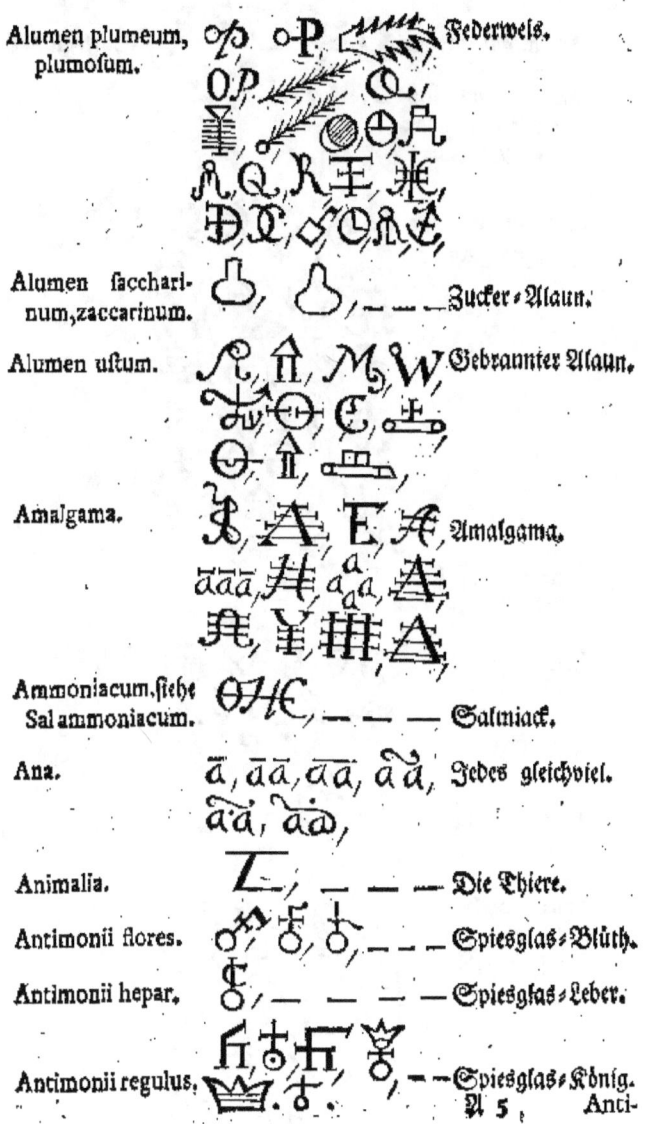

4

Antimonii vitrum.  Spiesglas-Glanz.

Antimonium, siehe antimonium spagyrice præpar:

Antimonium spagyr. præparatum. Spiesglas. Spiesglanz.

Aphronitrum, siehe Sal petrae.

Aqua. Wasser.

Aqua fontana. — — — Brunnen-Wasser.

Aqua fortis simplex, aqua gehennæ, stygia.

Aqua

Latin	Symbols	German
Aqua pluuialis.	▽ ▽ R ▽ ▽ R ▽	Regen-Waſſer
Aqua regis.	(symbols)	Goldſcheid-Waſſer.
Aqua vitae.	(symbols)	Aquavit, Lebens-Waſſer.
Arena.	(symbols)	Sand.
Argentum, luna.	(symbols)	Silber.

Argen-

6

Argentum folia- ⟨symbol⟩ — — — — Silber-Blättlein.
tum.

Argentum musi- ⟨symbols⟩ — — — Saiten-Silber.
cum.

Argentum picto- ⟨symbols⟩ — — — Mahler-Silber.
rium.

Argentum viuum, ⟨symbols⟩ Queck-Silber.
Mercurius viuus,
Hydrargyrum.

Armena bolus. ⟨symbol⟩ — — — — Armenischer Bolus.

Arsenicum album. ⟨symbols⟩ Weisser Arsenic,
Mauss-Gift, Ratten-Gift.

Arsenicum citri-
num, flauum lu- ⟨symbol⟩ — — — — Rauschgelb.
teum.   Arse-

Arsenicum rubrum Sandaracha graecorum.	[symbols]	Rauschgelb, rother Operment.
Arsenicum sublimatum.	[symbols]	Sublimirter Arsenick.
Atramentum, Vitriolum.	[symbols]	Dinte, Vitriol.
Atramentum album, Vitriolum album,	[symbols]	Kupfer-Waſſer, weiſſer Vitriol.
Aurichalcum, cuprum citrinum.	[symbols]	Meſſing.
Auripigmentum, Riſigallum.	[symbols]	Operment.

Aurum,

Aurum, Sol. [symbols] Gold.

Aurum foliatum. [symbol] — Gold-Blättlein.

Aurum muſicum. [symbols] Saiten-Gold.

Aurum pictorium. [symbols] — Mahler-Gold.

Aurum potabile. [symbols] — Trinckbar Gold.

Autumnus. [symbols] — Herbſt.

B.

Balneum. B, B, ℬ. — Bad.

Balneum arenæ. [symbols] Sandbad.

Balneum Mariae, Maris. MB, MB, BM, [symbols] Marienbad.

Balneum roris, vaporis. BR, VB. — Dampfbad.

Ben-

Benzoe flores, siehe Flores benzoe.		
Bezoar occidentalis.	⊖	West-Indischer Bezoar.
Bezoar orientalis.	⊙	Ost-Indischer Bezoar.
Bezoardicum Joviale.	♃	Schweistreibend Zinn.
Bezoardicum lunare.	☽	Schweistreibend Silber.
Bezoardicum martiale.	♂	Schweistreibend Eisen.
Bezoardicum minerale.	♀	Schweistreibender Spiesglas-König.
Bezoardicum Saturninum.	♄	Schweistreibend Bley.
Bezoardicum solare.	☉	Schweistreibend Gold.
Bezoardicum venereum.	♀	Schweistreibend Kupfer.
Bismuthum Marcasita.	⚒, ⚴	Wismuth.
Bolus alba.	⅍	Weisser Bolus.
Bolus armena, siehe armena bolus.		
Bolus communis.	d, ♂, ♋	Gemeiner Bolus. Borrax.

10

Latin	Symbols	German
Borax, Borrax.	[symbols]	Borax.
Cadmia factitia, fornacum, sihe	C.	Tutia, Tutien, Tuß.
Cadmia fossilis, pa- tiua, lapis cala- minaris.	[symbol]	Gallmey-Stein.
Calcinare.	[symbols]	Rösten, ausglühen, in ein Pulver ver- brennen.
Calcinatio argenti.	[symbols]	Das Ausglüen des Silbers in ein Pulver.
Calcinatio auri.	[symbol]	Das Ausglüen des Golds in ein Pul- ver.
Calx.	[symbols]	Kalch von Metallen.
Calx ouorum.	C qo.	Calcinirte Eyerscha- len.
Calx Solis.	[symbol]	Gold-Kalch.
Calx viua.	[symbols]	Ungelöschter Kalch.

Cam-

Camphora.	∞, ◇◇◇, ◇◇◇◇	Campher.
Cancer, astacus, Gammarus.	♋ — — — —	Ein Krebs.
Capella.	T P O X X	Sand-Capelle, Capelle.
Caput mortuum.	☉ ♏ ☽ ☉ ♃ ♀ ♈ ⊕ E ☉	Todtenkopf.
Catinus, tigillum.	▽ — — — —	Tiegel.
Caementare, stratificare.	⌂ ⚵ ⚶ ⚷ ⚸	Cämentiren.
Cera citrina.	(symbols) Æ	Gelb Wachs.
Cerussa, plumbago, plumbum album.	(symbols)	Bleyweiss.
Chalybs, ferrum.	(symbols) ♃ H₂	Stahl, Eisen.
Cineres clauellati, s. auch alkali sal.	⚇ ⚇ ⚇ VZ	Pottasche. Cin...

12.

Latin	Symbols	German
Cinis, cineres.		Asche.
Cinnabaris.		Zinnober.
Coagulatio.		Coaguliren.
Cobaltum.		Mucken-Gift.
Colaturae.	Col. Colat.	Das, was durchgeseyht, oder durchgesiegen ist.
Completus.	compl.	Das Complete.
Compositio.		Vermischung, Zusammensetzung vieler Artzneyen.
Cornu cerui.	CC	Hirschhorn.
Cornu cerui ustum.	CCV	Gebrannt Hirschhorn.
Cornuta.		Retorte.
Creta.		Kreide.
Crocus, crocus aromaticus.		Saffran.
Crocus martis.		Eisen-Saffran.

Crocus

Crocus meallorum.	[symbol]	Spiesglas-Saffran.
Crocus veneris.	[symbols]	Kupfer-Saffran.
Crucibulum, f. Catinus, und Tigillum.	[symbols]	Schmelz-Tiegel.
Cryſtallus.	[symbols]	Cryſtall.
Cucurbita.	CC	Ein gläſerner Kolbe.
Cucurbita cœca.	[symbol]	Ein blinder geſchloſſener Kolbe.
Cuprum, Venus, ſiehe aes.		
Cum vino.	C.V.	Mit Wein.

D.

Da & ſigna, oder detur, ſignetur.	D.S.	Gib und überſchreibe es.
Deſtillare, deſtillatio.	[symbols]	Brennen, deſtilliren.
Dies.	[symbols]	Tag.
Dies & nox, nyɛthemeron.	[symbols]	Tag und Nacht.

Di-

14

Digerere, digestio. ⟨symbols⟩ Digeriren, erwärmen.

Drachma, Holça. ℨ, ⟨symbol⟩ − − − Drachme, Quentlein; der vierte Theil eines Loths, 60. Gran, 3. Scrupel.

Drachma semis. ℨβ − − − − Ein halb Quentlein.

E.

Ebullitio. ⟨symbol⟩ − − − − Das Brausen, Sieden.

Elementa, principia corporum. ⟨symbols⟩ Die Grund-Theile der Cörper.

Essentia. ⟨symbol⟩ − − − − Eine Essenz.

Excipulum, siehe Receptaculum.

Extractio sicca. ⟨symbol⟩ Siehe Sublimatio, das Sublimiren.

F.

Farina. ⊙ − − − − Ein Mehl, feines Pulver.

Farina laterum. ⟨symbols⟩ Ziegel-Mehl.

Faex, faex vini, aceti. ⟨symbols⟩ − − Wein- oder Essig-Hefen.

Fel vitri, Sal vitri. ⟨symbols⟩ Glas-Galle.

Ferru-

Ferrugo, ferri vi-tium, situs.	☩, ♃ — — —	Eisen=Rost.
Ferrum, siehe Mars.	⚔, ⚒, ⚸, ♃, ♄, F, ♂, ⚹, ⚵	Eisen.
Filtratio, philtratio.	⌧, ◇, ⚹, 33, ♡, ⚱, ⚋	Das Filtriren durch-seihen, durch ein Lösch=Papier.
Filtrum, philtrum.	℔ — — — —	Ein Filtrir=Glas mit dem Zugehör.
Fimus, equinus.	℅, ℉, ℺, ⚔, ⚒, ♊, ♈, ⚸, ☉	Pferd=Mist oder an-dere feuchte Wär-me von Asche oder warmen Wasser zu dem Digeriren.
Fixus, fixum.	V̈ — — — —	Feuerbeständig.
Figere, fixatio.	V̈, ⚴, ≈, Ψ	Figiren, etwas Flüch-tiges Feuerbestän-dig machen.
Flores.	Fl. — — — —	Blumen.
Flores antimonii, siehe antimonii flores.		Spiesglas=Blu-men.
- - benzoe.	₨ — — — —	Benzoin=Blumen.
- - Martis, siehe crocus Martis.		Stahl=Blumen, Stahl=Saffran.

Flo-

16

Latin	Symbols	German
Flores vitrioli.	♄ – – –	Vitriol-Blumen.
Flores viridis aeris.	♃, ⚵ – –	Grünspan-Blumen.
Fluere.	⌇, ⚭, ♏, F,	Fließen.
Fornax, furnus.	▭, ⊙, ▫ – –	Ein Ofen.
Fuligo.	♌, ⌐, ℔, ✝,	Ruß.
Fumus.	⌑, ℓ, ∽ – –	Rauch.
Furnus, siehe Fornax.		
Fusio.	⊟y – –	Das Schmeltzen.

G.

Latin	Symbols	German
Gummi.	G, S, ℥, 8, ♋♋, ⚬, C, ♉♋, ♆♋,	Ein Gummi, Hartz.
Gummi arabicum.	匚 – – –	Arabischer Gummi.
Gradatio.	Mav, J, Mra	Das Gradiren, Erhöhen der Metalle.
Gradus ignus.	♌ – – –	Grad des Feuers.
Granatus.	✠ – – –	Granat-Stein.
Granum.	gr. – – –	Ein Gran, der 60ste Theil eines Quintleins, oder 20ste einer Scrupel. Gut-

Gutta. guttae.	G. g. gtt — — —	Ein Tropfen; Tropfen.

H.

Haematites, siehe Lapis haematites.		
Herba.	H, HB — — —	Ein Kraut.
Hermetice sigillatum.	H. S. — — —	Hermetisch sigillirt, zugeschmelzt.
Hora.	⧖, 1ʰ, A, II, ⎾⏌, Ə, H, ✳, ∀, ⊞, ⏽ —	Eine Stunde.
Hiems.		Der Winter.
Hydrargyrum, siehe Argentum vivum.		

I.

Ignis.	△, △, □, Z, ♒20	Das Feuer.
Ignis circulatorius.	△, ⊖, C, A — —	Ein gelind, Circulir Feuer.
Ignis fortis.	⌒⌒, △△ — — —	Ein stark Feuer.
Ignis lentus.	☫, △, ⊼, L△	Ein langsam, gelind Feuer.
Ignis reuerberius.	⩕ — — —	Ein Reverberir Feuer.
Ignis rotae.	⊙ — — — —	Ein Rad-Feuer.
Imbibere.	✡ — — — —	Träncken.

B 4   In-

18

Incompletus.	Inc. P. incompl	Das Incomplete.
Jupiter, ſtannum.	♃ ♃ ⚹ ⚭, ...	Zinn.

L.

Lege artis.	ℒ a. l. a.	Nach der Kunſt.
Lamina.	▱, ▭	— Ein Blech.
Lana illota, Erion.	HS	— Ungewaſchene Wolle.
Lapides.	V, ⊞, Ɣ, ✝, ∈,	Steine.
Lapis armenius, armenus, Malachites.	℞	— Armenien-Stein, Bergblau.
Lapis bezoar occidentalis, ſ. Bezoar occidental.		
- - - - Orientalis, ſ. Bezoar orientalis.		
- - calaminaris, ſ. Calaminaris.	E	— Gallmey-Stein. Kalk-Stein.
- - calcarius.		
- - haematites.		Blut-Stein.
- - Lazuli.		Laſur-Stein. Lapis

Lapis Magnes, Sideritis Plinii, Lapis nauticus.	♂, ☍ ✠ ⚴	Magnet-Stein, Magnet, Segel-Stein.
Lapis fabulosus; osteocolla.	〰️	— Bein-Bruch.
Lapis silex.	∘∘∘	— Kiesel, Kiesel-Stein.
Later.	▦, ▭, ▨	— Ziegel-Stein.
Lateres cribrati.	▦, ▭, ▭, ▭, ▦	Gesiebte Ziegel-Steine.
Libra.	℔ ℔ ⚖ ℔, ♎ ♃ 24 ℔	Ein Pfund.
Libra ciuilis, pondus ciuile.	c. p.	Ein gemein Pfund von 32. Loth.
Libra medicinalis.	m. p.	Ein Apotheker-Pfund von 24. Loth oder 12. Onzen.
Libra pensilis.	⚖	— Eine Wage.
Lignum.	⚓, ♀	— Holz.
Limatura chalybis, martis.	↯, ○→, ♂	Feil-Staub, Eisenfeil.
Lixiuium, siehe auch alcali.	♅ ♃ ℒ ♄	Eine Lauge, ein Laugen-Salz.

E 5   Lu-

20

Luna, siehe Argentum. — Silber.

Lutatio. △, ≈ ⏑ N N — Das Verlutiren, Verklaiben der Gefässe.

Lutum. Z, C — — — — Ein Leim oder Kütt.

Lutum Philosophorum, lutum sapientiae. ℈ Z, ♃, •−⊖−•, F, LN — Der philosophische Leim oder Kütt.

Magnes, siehe Lapis magnes. M.

Manipulus, Mannes. M, man. — — — Eine Handvoll.

Magnesia. ⊙—♄, M, ⊅ — Magnesien.

Marcasita, siehe Bismuthum. ⚯, ⛰, ⊥, ♂ ♂ Marcasit, Wismuth. M, ♃, ♀, V ⊞, ⊖, Ψ, →, ♋,

Marcasita aurea, oder metallica, siehe Zincum. ⊞, ⊞ — — — Zinck.

Mars, siehe Ferrum. ▫, ♃, ♂, ⚹, ♀, ⚶ Eisen. ♂, S,

Massa,

Massa.	⌀ ⟳ ⌀	Eine Masse oder ein Taig zu Pflastern, Pillen.
Massa pilularum.	M	Eine Pillen-Masse.
Materia.	ã a, maa	Eine Materie.
Materia prima.	⚴, ▢, °°°	Eine Grund-Materie.
Mel.	M, ☉, ✿, ⚹, ⧉, ⧠, H, 秊, ⚹	Honig.
Mensis.	⊠ ⊠, ♃, ⌇, ⊠	Ein Monat.
Mercurius viuus, s. Hydrargyrum, argentum viuum.	☿	
Mercurius praecipitatus albus.	☿⇌, ☿, ⨍ ☿, ☿ ...	Weisser Präcipitat von Queck-Silber.
Mercurius praecipitatus ruber.	☿. r	Rother Präcipitat.
Mercurius Saturni praecipitatus, Minium.	... 8, 85. ... ⋀, ...	Mening, Mini.
Mercurius sublimatus.	... ... , ♏, 1, 85, ... ⋀, ...	Sublimat.

Mi-

Minium, sihe Mer-
 curius Saturni
 praecipitatus.   Mening, Mini.

Misce, NB. am En-   *M.* — — —   Mische.
 de der Recepte.

Mixtura simplex   *M. S L.*   —D. Ludwigs simple
 Ludouici.   Tropfen.

N.

Numero.   *Nr. N°.* — —   An der Zahl. Wird
                                             z. E. gebraucht,
                                             wo man Früchte
                                             verschreibt.

Nitrum commune.   Salpeter.

Nox.   Eine Nacht.

Nux moschata.   *NM* — — — —   —Muscatnuß.

Nycthemeron, sihe   Tag und Nacht.
 dies & nox.

O.

Obulus scrupulus ℈ß — — — — —   Ein halber Scrupel
 semis,   oder 10. Gran.
                                                        Oleum

Oleum.	♁,	— — — — Oel.
Oleum commune, oleum oliuarum, gremiale.	⟨symbols⟩	Baum-Oel.
Oleum Saturni.	⟨symbols⟩	Bley-Oel.
- - Sulphuris.	⟨symbols⟩	Schwefel-Oel.
- - Talchi oder Talci.	⟨symbols⟩	Talck-Oel.
- - Tartari Sennerti.	⟨symbols⟩	D. Sennerts Weinstein-Oel.
- - Vitrioli.	⟨symbols⟩	Vitriol-Oel.
Ouum.	⟨symbols⟩	Ein Ey.
Pars cum parte.	P. ⟨symbols⟩	Eine Masse von gleichviel Gold und Silber untereinander cämentirt und graduirt.
Per deliquium.	p d.	Von selbst zerflossen.
Phlegma, aqua insipida.	⟨symbols⟩	Ein unschmackhaftes Wasser.
Piscis, ichthys.	♓. ⟨symbol⟩	Ein Fisch.
Plumbago, plumbum album, siehe Cerussa.	⟨symbols⟩	Bleyweis.
Plumbum, Saturnus.	⟨symbols⟩	Bley.

Prae-

24

Praecipitatio, praecipitatus.	≈ – – –	Niedergeschlagen, gefällt.
Praeparatio, praeparatus.	ƿƿᵗ – – – –	Präparirt.
Pugillus.	P. ⫶⫶⫶ p. – –	Ein Pugill, was man zwischen 3. Finger fassen kann.
Pugillus semis.	Pß ⫶⫶⫶ p.ß. –	Eine halbe Pugill, oder auch so viel man zwischen 2. Finger fassen kan.
Puluis.	Pulv. ✚, ⊥, ⅙, ℟,	Ein Pulver.
Pulueriſare.	A, ✖, ⫶, ✚)	(Zu Pulver zerstoſſen.)
Purificatio.	℧ ℧ ℧ ℧ ℧	Die Reinigung.
Putredo, putrefactio.	ⵄ ✚, ⵄ ES, ⟁	Die Fäulung, das Verfaulen.

Q.

Quantum placet.	q. pl. – – –	So viel beliebt.
Quantum ſatis.	q. ſ. – – –	Bis es genug iſt.
– – – uis.	q. v. – – –	So viel man will.
Quinta eſſentia.	Q. E. – – –	Die Quint-Eſſenz, das feineſte und beſte. Ra-

R.

Radix, radices.	*Rad.* — —	Wurzeln.
Rasura, raspatum.	*Ras. R. rasur. rasp.*	Etwas Geraspeltes.
Realgar. fumus, exhalatio & concretio.	♆, ♂, ⚸, ♃, ✕, ♃, ♄, ⚬⚬⚬	Ein Rauch, der sich wieder in eine trockene Materie zusammengesetzt hat.
Receptaculum, Recipiens, excipulum.	♃, ⚿ — —	Ein Recipient, oder Glas, das man bey Destillationen vorschlägt, um das herübergehende abzufassen.
Receptum, formula medica, recepta.	*Recept.*	Ein Recept.
Recipe.	℞, ℞, ℞, ℥, ♃	Nimm, NB. wird vornenhin auf den Recepten gesetzt.
Reductio.	*V, V, E* — —	Die Reduction, oder Wiederbringung in die vorige Gestalt.
Regulus.	♕, ♛, — —	Ein Metall-König.
Regulus antimonii medicinalis.	☿̑ — — — —	Der Arzney Spiesglas König.
Renouatio metallorum.	⚶ — — — —	Die Erneurung der zerstörten Metalle.
		Resina.

26

Resina.	⚶ _ _ _ _ _	—Ein Harz.
Retorta, cornuta, matracium.	6, 6, 6, 6 _	Eine Retorte, Elephanten-Schnabel.
Reuerberatio.	♃ ♃ ♃ ⚯ ⚴, R	Das Reverberiren.
Reuerberatorium, reuerberium.	♄, ♃ _ _ _ _	Ein Reverberir-Ofen.
Rhabarbarum.	*Rhab.* _ _ _	Rhabarbara.
Risigallum, siehe Auripigmentum.		
	𝑆	
Saccharum.	Σ _ _ _ _ _	—Zucker.
Sal.	⊖ _ _ _ _ _	—Salz.
Sal alcali, oder alkali, s. alcali und Cineres clauellati.	♀ ♃ ⚵ ⚱, X, 8, G, ⊞, F, E, ⊦, ⚶, ⋏, ⋏, R, ⚸ ⚶ ⚶ O4 L A, ⚶ ⚶ ⚶ ⚶,	Laugen-Salz, Potasche.
Sal ammoniacum oder armoniacum.	⊖ Ec. ✳ ⊙ ♆ ✶, F, ∞, Z, ⚹, S,)C OIC ...., ♆ X ♄ ♆, X, M ✳ ⚶ ⟡ ⚶ X,)C,	Salmiack.

74

Sal commune.	[alchemical symbols]	Gemein Saltz, Kuchen-Saltz.
Sal colcotharium, vitriolum vomitiuum.	[symbol] — — —	Vitriol-Saltz.
Sal essentiale vini, siehe Terra foliata tartari.		
Sal gemmae, oder fossile, indum.	[alchemical symbols]	Stein-Saltz.
Sal marinum.	[symbols] — —	Meer-Saltz.
Sal petrae, aphronitrum, flos parietis, faex nitri, Nitrum Graecorum, Nitrum stolidum.	[symbols]	Mauren- oder Keller-Salpeter.

C   Sal

28

Sal Tartari fixum.	⚹ ⚹ ⚹ ⚹ ⚹ ⚹ ⚹	Weinstein-Saltz.
Sal essentiale, s. Terra foliata tartari. Sal vini essentiale.	⚹ ⚹ ⚹	ist wieder das vorige.
Sal volatile.	θV. θΛ. — —	Ein flüchtig. Saltz.
Sal urinae.	⚹, ⊙, ⊡, ⊟	Urin, Harn-Saltz.
Sapo.	◇, ⚹ — —	Seiffe.
Saturnus, s. plumbum.	⚹, ♄, 5, 5, ♃ ♓, ⚹,	Bley.
Scriptulus und Scripulus.		ist so viel als Scrupulus.
Scrupulus.	Ɉ, Ↄ, F — —	Ein Scrupel, 20. Gran.
Secundum artem.	S. a, S. A. —	—Nach der Kunst.
Semen, Semina.	Sem. — — —	—Saamen.
Semis, semissis.	S. β. — — —	Halb.
Semiuncia, semuncia, uncia semis oder dimidia.	ʒ β. ʒiv — —	Eine halbe Onz, ein Loth oder 4. Quintlein.
Sextarius.	⚹, Ew, ⚹, — —	Ein Sextarius.

Sicca-

Siccare.	𝒟. — — — —	Trocknen.
Siccum.	𝒮 — — —	Trocken.
Signa, signetur.	𝒮 — — —	überschreibe es.
Simplex & compositum.	𝒮. et C. —	Einfach und zusammengesetzt.
Sine vino.	𝒮.𝑣. — —	Ohne Wein.
Sine stipitibus.	𝒮𝒮. — — —	Ohne Stiele.
Soda.	⊔ — —	Spanischer Sod.
Sol, s. aurum.	☩, ⚔, ⚒, ☉, ⚘, 🜚, E⚭, ˢE, V, E, 𝒮2, F, L, Z, 7,	
Solutio, soluere.	∽, 𝒥𝒱, 𝒮°, 𝒮𝓋,	Das Solviren, Auflösen.
Species.	𝒮pec. — —	Species.
Spiritus.	𝒮p. 𝒮pir, ⌒, ⚯, Ein Geist. ⚵, ⚶, ⊃⊂, S, 🜍, ⚴, ⊖, ✳	
Spiritus vini. Spiritus vini rectificatissimus, siehe Alcohol vini.	1ˢ, V/m, ♏︎, ⚯, V, ♀, ⚹, ⚛, ☥, 2↯, ⚘,	Brandwein.
Stannum, siehe Jupiter.		

Stra-

Stratum super stratum.	SSS, ⚏, sSS✝	Ein Stratum super Stratum.
Sublimatio, sublimare.	(symbols)	Sublimiren, sublimirt.
Succinum album, Leucelectrum.	BS, SVA, S.V.A	Weißer Agtstein.
Succus.	(symbol) — — —	Ein Saft.
Sulphur.	(symbols)	Schwefel.
Sulphur nigrum.	(symbols)	Der schwarze Schwefel.
Sulphur philosophorum.	(symbols)	Der philosophische Schwefel.
Sulphur stillatitium.	(symbol) — — —	Tropf-Schwefel.
Sulphur tartari, tinctura sulphuris.	(symbol) — —	Weinstein-Tinctur.
Sulphur viuum.	(symbols) — —	Lebendiger Schwefel.

Tal-

T.

Talca, Talcum.   ⚹ X ⊕ ♃ ♄,   Talch, Talck.

Tartarus.   [alchemical symbols]   Weinstein.

Tartarus emeticus.   ♀ E, – – – – Brech=Weinstein,

Tauri priapus.   8 ४. – – – – Ein Ochsenziemmer, oder Farrenschwantz.

Terebinthina.   [symbols] – – – – Terpenthin, Claret, Lerchen=Hartz.

Terra.   [symbols]   Erde.

Terra foliata tartari.   [symbols]   Weinstein=Saltz mit Essig getrånckt.

Terra Lemnia.   [symbols]   Gesiegelte Erde von der Insel Lemno.

C 3   Terra

34

Terra figillata alba. — Weiſſe geſiegelte Erde.

Tigillum, ſ. Crucibulum. — Ein Tiegel.

Tinctura. — Eine Tinctur.

Turbithum, Turpethum minerale. — Mineral-Turpeth.

Tutia Alexandrina.
Tutia Officinarum,
Cadmia factitia,
Cadmia fornacum. — Tutien, Tutſus, grauer Hüttenrauch.

U.

Uncia. 85, 33, — Eine Onz, 2. Loth, 8. Quentlein.

Uncia ſemis. — Eine halbe Onz, ein Loth.

Urina, lotium. — Urin, Harn.

Vaporis

Vaporis balneum, fiehe Balneum roris.	V.	
Venus cuprum, fiehe auch aes.	♁ ♃ ♀ L C ⚥ ♀ ♀ ♂ ⚲ ÷ ▢ ♀	Kupfer.
Ver.	♀ — — —	Der Frühling.
Vesica destillatoria.	X, ⚹ — — —	Eine Destillir-Blase.
Vinum.	V, †, ☽, ☺ —	Wein.
Vinum adustum, spiritus frumenti.	⚝, ⊙ — — —	Frucht-Brandwein.
Vinum album.	2, VA, ∪, ⚏, ⚝, ⚘	Weisser Wein.
Vinum alcalisatum, oder circulatum, correctum.		ist so viel als Alcohol vini.
Vinum emeticum.	VE — — — —	Ein Brech-Wein.
Vinum Hippocraticum.	VH, VH —	Ein Hippocras-Wein.
Vinum medicatum.	VM — — —	Ein Kräuter-Wein.
Vinum mortuum, s. acetum.	⊙, M, ⚴ — —	Essig.
Vinum rubrum.	VR — — — —	Rother-Wein.

24

Viride aeris, viride [symbols] Grünspan.
graecum. oder hi-
spanicum.

Vitellus, Luteum, [symbols] Eyerdotter, das Gel-
Luteum oui. be des Eys.

Vitriolum, f. auch [symbols] Vitriol, Kupfer-
atramentum. Waſſer.

Vitriolum album. [symbols] Weſſer Vitriol, Ca-
lizel-Stein.

Vitriolum Roma- [symbols] Römiſcher Vitriol.
num.

Vitrum. [symbols] Glas.

Vitrum antimonii,
ſiehe antimonii
vitrum.

Volatile. [symbols] Flüchtig.

Zincum, Zinctum, [symbol]
Zinck, Zink, ſiehe
Marcaſita aurea.
Zingiber. [symbols] Ingber.
Zinziber.

NB.

The Seals (Sigils) of the Goetia

One thing we have to remember about alchemy is while it was a philosophy meant to help a person perform the inner great work, it also manifested tangibly in laboratory alchemy which birthed modern chemistry. In magick, we're attempting to perform the inner great work in hopes that it manifests tangibly in the world around us. Whether that's changing our perspective or inner dialogue, it holds true that even high magick that manifests internally is bound to manifest externally in some way and hopefully vice-versa. It's simply up to us to recognize this in our day-to-day mundane lives.

That co-worker you think is a jerk may simply be a test of your inner alchemy work. The more often you consider how rather mundane things are actually part of our great work, the more you will be able to see the benefits of that work and live a spiritual life on a day-to-day basis. The following pages hold my personal insights into the alchemy and symbolism of the seals of the Goetic Spirits, for your consideration.

Please remember that it's important to decipher alchemical

symbolism in relation to the material that accompanies the images.

That said, it's important to keep in mind that there are five stages of the alchemical process:

Nigredo – the blackening, the state of darkness, often associated with depression when dealing with psychology.
Albedo – the whitening or the stage of enlightenment
Rubedo - the red stage where passion and sacrifice enter the great work.
Solutio- when the matter is dissolved.
Separatio - where the contents are separated and taken apart and examined.

Psychologically speaking, since shadow work is a process of inner psychological work, it goes something like this: You are in a dark place (Nigredo – the blackening), you realize you're in a dark place and things need to change (Albedo – the whitening - enlightenment), and you begin to work on the figuring out why you're in a dark place and go about correcting it (Rubedo). Solutio and Separatio are "correction" stages, where you do the work to make the change.

During the transformative stage, beginning at *rubedo*, there are seven steps (not be confused with the 12 alchemical processes, each associated with an astrological sign):

1. Calcination
2. Dissolution
3. Separation
4. Conjunction
5. Fermentation
6. Distillation
7. Coagulation

7 is the number of the spiritual. A union of the physical 4 to the divine 3.

Speaking of numbers, there is a lot of numerology at play in the descriptions of the spirits themselves, too, being that each spirit rules over rather specific numbers of legions. I do not go into that here. You can look up, for example, the meaning of the number 66 in Crowley's *Liber 777* and apply that to Bael on your own. Or do basic numerology where 6 + 6 = 12, and 1 + 2 = 3 and then look up the meaning for the number three. (See *Foundational Correspondences for Daemonolaters* for the meaning of 1-9.) Dealing with the alchemical symbolism, color, and imagery was task enough without throwing numerology in there, too. However, the numerology in the descriptions might be a good homework assignment for the studious magician who wants to dig a little deeper. (Hint, hint.) If I'm feeling ambitious, perhaps you'll see a *Numerology of Goetia* as another book in my Goetia series at some point.

It might be also important to note that the seals of angelic and other spirits from the other four books in the Lemegeton (The Lesser Key of Solomon) also contain alchemical symbolism to outline processes, recipes, and inner alchemical work. The seals/sigils have also been referred to as *emblems* by alchemists.

The twelve alchemical processes and their zodiac signs:

1. **Calcination** (Aries)
2. **Congelation** (Taurus)
3. **Fixation** (Gemini)
4. **Dissolution** (Cancer)
5. **Digestion** (Leo)

6. **Distillation** (Virgo)
7. **Sublimation** (Libra)
8. **Separation** (Scorpio)
9. **Ceration** (Sagittarius)
10. **Fermentation** (Capricorn)
11. **Multiplication** (Aquarius)
12. **Projection** (Pisces)

How the Seals are Broken Down

The following image is an example of how I broke down each seal. One by one, I went through each symbol and tried to find matches.

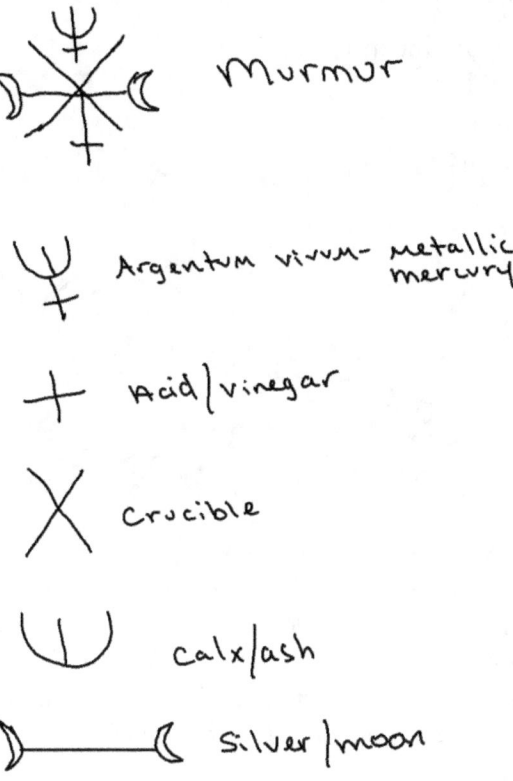

Now, on to the spirits of the Ars Goetia.

1: Bael

KING

Color: Yellow.
Incense: Frankincense.
Metal: Gold.
Planet: Sun
Element: Fire

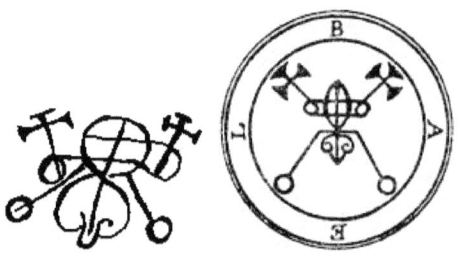

*The first principal spirit is a king ruling in the East, called **Bael**. He makes men go invisible, he rules over 66 legions of inferior spirits, he appears in diverse shapes, sometimes like a cat, sometimes like a toad, sometimes like a man, and sometimes in all these forms at once. He speaks in a hoarse voice.*

The Alchemical Breakdown:

While the seal seems very insect or frog-like (transformation), notice the mention of cats (transformation of hidden knowledge). Within the sigil itself we see the alchemical symbol for day, nitrum soda, gold pigment, and potentially alum, the process of digestion, and acetum. In alchemy, the process of digestion involves applying a heat source to the material over the period of several weeks. It is one of the 12 core processes of alchemical work. It's interesting that the symbol for digestion is contained within the seal, and invisibility is mentioned in the description for Bael. Bael appears to be an active force and can help the magician transform physical energy into creative energy with the end goal being manifestation. When we heat something slowly, especially something solid immersed in liquid, it releases the essence of the physical matter into the liquid around it. Acid can spur this process, as in digestion.

In spiritual alchemy, you might even consider this a process of emotional release. Bael is a reminder that transformation begins within the wellspring of our deepest emotions and that what we digest makes manifest our situation in the external world. If, for example, we consume nothing but negative media, we begin to feel negative and that manifests in our everyday life until life becomes negative. If we feel invisible to others and begin to see ourselves as invisible, we become invisible.

I am inclined to believe this may be a recipe to make gold pigment. To "paint" situations with gold perhaps? The phrase, *fake it until you make it* comes to mind. That said, it could also be a recipe for making a white elixir from alum and gold by digestion that is said to be able to change any metal to silver of all things. Not gold.

2: Agares

DUKE

Color: Green.
Incense: Sandalwood.
Metal: Copper.
Planet: Venus
Element: Earth

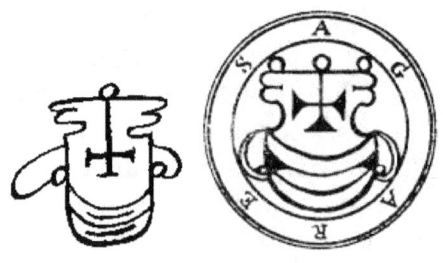

*The second spirit is a Duke called **Agares**. He is under the power of the East and comes up in the form of a fair old man riding upon a crocodile, very mildly, carrying a hawk on his fist. He makes those who run that stand still, and fetches back runaways. He can teach all languages or tongues presently. He has the power also to destroy dignities, both supernatural and temporal; and can cause earthquakes. He was of the Order of Virtues; he has under his government 31 Legions. His seal is to be worn as a lamen.*

The Alchemical Breakdown:

The earthy part of air, Agares' seal combines symbols of purification and calcination, and contains the alchemical symbol for copper, which when oxidized, turns green (hence why we use green for copper). The overall symbolism appears to be purification through calcination, one of the first processes of alchemy. Calcination occurs when extreme heat is applied to matter, turning it into a fine white ash called salt. It is a means of purifying the physical ingredient for an elixir.

Notice that crocodiles (Agares rides upon a messenger of the gods) and hawks (element air, communication, intelligence, spiritual awareness) are mentioned here. Agares as a messenger of the divine, brings spiritual awareness to the magician. As well as creativity, the skills to communicate, and wisdom. He causes runaways to stand still. To discover what they're running from and to learn communication instead of fleeing. He can cause the magician to question his worth spiritually, and physically (both uncomfortable things many people run away from) and can bring a calm mind and the ability to analyze ourselves.

This can manifest as better communication with others, being a better partner or friend, and can even help us grow and face our fears instead of running from them. Many seek Agares for wise counsel and advice for all manner of things.

This purification through calcination process, however, may involve reducing the magician to ash so that we can be purified of bad habits or our own egocentrism. I've said it many times, Daemons are lesson teachers, and sometimes, in order for us to pay attention, we need the world around us to burn in order for us to rebuild a better world/life for ourselves.

3: Vassago

PRINCE

Color: Blue.
Incense: Cedar.
Metal: Tin.
Planet: Jupiter.
Element: Water

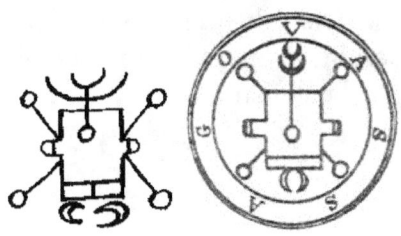

The Third spirit is a mighty prince, being of the same nature as Agares, he is called **Vassago**. *This spirit is of a good nature, and his office is to declare things past and to come; and to discover all things hidden or lost. He governs 26 legions of spirits.*

The Alchemical Breakdown:

Vassago's seal, despite the spirit's brief description, seems to embody a rather complex alchemical operation that involves both day and night operations meant to both distill and solidify the emotional mind. Even though his metal is tin (the symbol for tin is present in the seal) and the planetary aspect Jupiter, there are symbols for both mercury and the moon contained in the seal. There is an airy – watery combination working within the seal, suggesting making a distillate of some kind.

The process of distillation of something solid is at work here. In the context of high magick, we could be looking at a process where the magician takes a deep dive into his emotions and thoughts that are rigid. Ideas he may be reluctant to give up because they are beliefs he holds dear and true. In letting go of these things through distilling them – we can see more clearly and gain insight (divination, intuition) and can more clearly see what we need to see (find hidden things). By distilling these thoughts, the magician then creates new beliefs and ideas that become solidified in place of the initial matter we started with before the distillation.

4: Gamigin

MARQUIS

Color: Violet
Incense: Jasmine
Metal: Silver
Planet: Moon
Element: Water
(Also Samigina)

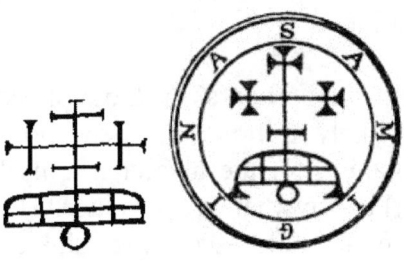

The 4th spirit is called **Gamigin**, a great Marquis. He appears in the form of a little horse or ass, and then into human shape. He puts himself at the request of the magician and speaks with a hoarse voice. He teaches all the liberal sciences and gives an account of the dead souls of them that die in sin. He rules over 30 legions of inferiors. Gamigin's seal is to be worn by the magician when he invokes this spirit.

The Alchemical Breakdown:

The seal appears to be outlining the operation of a spagyric preparation of vinegar of antimony starting with the distillation of the vinegar. The symbolism is all there, and the symbols for gold, the crucible, and aluminum are also present despite Gamigin (also Samagina) having silver as the ruling metal. Spagyric operations include warming the preparation in the sun (or within horse dung), as an operation of the daytime. Usually, to create vinegar of antimony, a tincture is extracted from a glass substance formed by roasting stibnite at high temperatures and condensing the fumes that form. The resulting vinegar of antimony is a yellowish pigment used for porcelain and glassware coloring.

If we look at this process in the context of spiritual alchemy, it's likely a process where prismatic crystals (perhaps a metaphor for the magician himself) are roasted (put to the test) to see what they produce. This is much like throwing one in the pool to see if they sink or swim. In the magician's case, perhaps this is indicative of throwing one into a great emotional turmoil to see if one can navigate it.

In the description, it says he appears as a little horse, or an ass. In alchemy, horses are representative of the four elements, suggesting balance or a need to find balance.

5: Marbas

PRESIDENT

Color: Orange
Incense: Storax
Metal: Mercury
Planet: Mercury
Element: Air

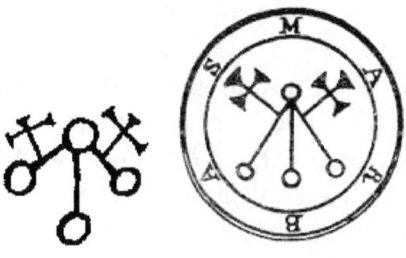

*The 5th spirit is called **Marbas** -- he is a great president and appears at first in the form of a great lion: but afterwards puts on human shape. At the request of the magician, he answers truly of things hidden or secret. He causes diseases and cures them again and gives great wisdom and knowledge in the mechanical arts, and changes men into other shapes. He governs 36 legions of spirits.*

The Alchemical Breakdown:

The sigil of Marbas looks rather simple and indicates the distillation of vinegar or acid. The distillation of vinegar or acid in alchemy was a way of extracting the hidden essence and properties of metals, as well as creating new substances with different qualities.

Marbas is described as a great lion and represents gold and ascension or enlightenment. Lions were protectors of alchemical secrets. In the context of the spirit in question he uncovers secrets, and both causes and heals illnesses. He also allegedly deals with the mechanical arts. It makes me think of how we can sometimes create our own illnesses and problems by our own negative thought patterns and what (and who) we surround ourselves with. This distillation process is meant to remove impurities (illnesses) via distillation to bring about good health and keep our minds and bodies in good working order.

Notice I mention the mind. Air is the element of mental faculties and is a reminder that our mental health is just as important as our physical and emotional health. They're all interconnected. This also reminds me of people who may take internally a teaspoon of red wine vinegar daily to improve their health or vitality. Yes, there are people who do this.

6: Valefor

DUKE

Color: Green
Incense: Sandalwood
Metal: Copper
Planet: Venus
Element: Earth

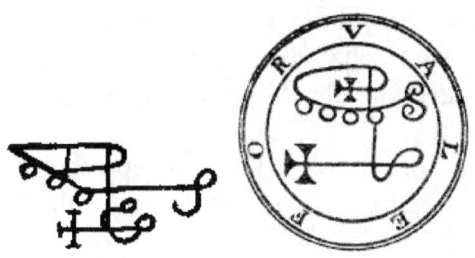

The 6th spirit is **Valefar.** He is a Mighty Duke, and appears in the form of a lion with a man's head. He is a good familiar, but tempts those he is familiar with to steal. He governs 10 legions of spirits. His seal is to be worn constantly if you are familiar with him, otherwise not.

The Alchemical Breakdown:

The seal of Valefor contains symbolism for the moon and silver, to dissolve something in a solution, the symbol for Venus, the symbol for oil, and the symbol for acid. It is a process of dissolution. Because this is a demon of earth and we have the symbolism of the Moon, it suggests dissolving emotional barriers that may be affecting the physical body. The description of the demon suggests the demon brings good familiars and tempts magicians to steal. I'm thinking perhaps emotions like envy and covetous desires. To bring them to a head and dissolve them. The representation of both the moon and silver also suggests an intuitive and perhaps even psychic connection that can affect physical matter. which would explain why this demonic force would also be good to obtain familiars, because of that psychic link.

Some possible recipes that contain these ingredients include recipes for purple and green pigments, for painting, as well as a white elixir from silver and oil by dissolution, which allegedly can allegedly turn any metal to silver.

Valefor also appears as a lion, to represent gold and the individual ascension and enlightenment of the alchemist.

7: Amon

MARQUIS

Color: Violet
Incense: Jasmine
Metal: Silver
Planet: Moon
Element: Water

*The 7th spirit is **Amon**. He is a Marquis great in power and most strong. He at first appears like a wolf with a serpent's tail, vomiting out of his mouth flames of fire, but at the command of the magician he puts on the shape of a man with dogs teeth beset in a head like a raven, or in a ravens head. He tells all things past and to come, and procures love, and reconciles controversies between friends and foes. He governs 40 legions of spirits.*

The Alchemical Breakdown:

Amon is true to water demons in that his seal contains all of the elements of intuition and psychic knowledge along with emotional intelligence. Not only does the seal encompass symbols of silver and the Moon but also suggests layers of silver. The S on the right-hand side appears to be mirrored on the left-hand side. That S looks like the symbol for silver and the Moon but in the encircled sigil it looks like the symbol for lead. The seal overall looks to be the dissolution of emotion, or an operation meant to dissolve something in a liquid solution.

So, dissolving psychic barriers between the past, present, and future, or to dissolve strife between friends and foes. Which makes complete sense according to his description.

In the description it mentions he appears like a wolf. Wolves, in alchemy, are symbolic of antimony – the metal in alchemy used to purify gold. Wolves also represent the need to tame the sometimes savage nature of the alchemical process. Translating that to spiritual alchemy, the wolf suggests the need to tame our savage instincts and emotions that may cause more harm than good.

8: Barbatos

DUKE

Color: Green
Incense: Sandalwood
Metal: Copper
Planet: Venus
Element: Fire

*The 8th spirit is called **Barbatos**. He is a great duke and appears when the sun is in Sagittarius. With four noble kings and their companions in great troops, he gives the understanding of the singing of birds, and the voice of other creatures and the barking of dogs. He breaks hidden treasures open, that have been laid by the enchantment of magicians. He is of the order of virtues, which some part bear rule still and he knows all things past and to come and reconciles friends and those that are in power. He rules over 30 Legions of spirits.*

The Alchemical Breakdown:

The process this sigil appears to be describing is one where acid is applied to copper to create the green rust, copper acetate. In the sigil on the right, it appears that there is a repetition of the process multiple times as the symbol of repetition appears, with multiple suggestions of tempering fire with water. The symbol for fire appears 6 times in the sigil on the right, four on the sigil to the left (the up facing triangle). The symbol for acid appears three times in each sigil – which also supports this repetition. It feels like a recipe for tempering metal.

Now, in context of the text, there is some suggested psychic ability with Barbatos, which is usually a quality of water, but fire can also bring creativity and bright flashes of insight and psychic ability. So, this tempering fire with water, or copper with acid, makes sense. Especially with regard to breaking hidden treasures open in that wonderful metaphoric sense medieval magicians loved so much.

The mention of birds in the description, "the understanding of the singing of birds" suggests the understanding of spiritual transformation of the alchemist. And "the voice of other creatures and the barking of dogs" may suggest a deeper understanding of the alchemical process leading to both spiritual and emotional intelligence.

9: Paimon

KING

Color: Yellow
Incense: Frankincense
Metal: Gold
Planet: Sun
Element: Water

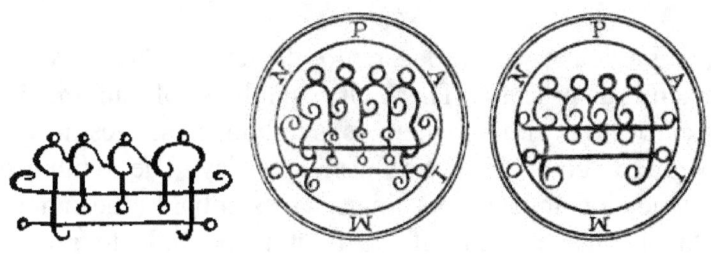

The 9*th* spirit in order is **Paimon,** *a great king, and very obedient to Lucifer. He appears in the form of a man, sitting on a camel [dromedary], with a Crown most glorious on his head. There goes before him a host of spirits like men with trumpets and well sounding cymbals, and all other sorts of musical instruments. He hath a great voice, and roars at his first coming, and his speech is such as the magician cannot well understand, unless he compels him. This spirit can teach all arts and sciences, and other secret things. He can discover what the Earth is, and what holds it up in the waters, and what the wind is or where it is, or any other thing you desire to know. He gives dignity and confirms the same. He binds or makes a man subject to the magician if he desires it, He gives good*

*familiars, and such as can teach all art. He is to be observed towards the northwest. He is of the order of dominions and has 200 Legions of spirits under him, one part of them is of the order of angels and the other of potentates. If you call this spirit Paimon alone you must make some offering to him and there will attend him 2 kings called **Bebal** and **Abalam**, and other spirits of the order of potentates in his host are 25 Legions because all those spirits which are subject to him, are not always with him unless the Magician compels them.*

The Alchemical Breakdown:

This particular seal appears to depict a more involved alchemical process. There are symbols of sublimation repeated four times. There is symbolism suggesting the operation should be done during the day. The symbol of liquefication appears four times. The symbol of the sun and gold are also present. It's also quite possible to see the symbolism of distillation there. Four times distilled. It really depends on the seal you're looking at.

In those four curly cues – it looks to be symbolic of repeated sublimation. In another seal, it looks like liquefication. And in the third, it looks like a repeated distillation. It's also quite possible that these could be symbols of cinnabar or even quintessence. That is a lot of information to work with.

The recipe appears to deal with transmutation of metals as most alchemical recipes do. One recipe to make an elixir of cinnabar and gold is said to transmute all metals. Where another recipe creates a white elixir solution of mercury and gold (despite no mercury used) that allegedly turns any metal to silver.

Paimon, in his description, teaches all arts and sciences in the occult, can be invoked to bind others, and we can look at these two things as deep emotional processes. A more modern interpretation of this particular spirit suggests one would work with Paimon for emotional intelligence and to heal deep trauma. This makes complete sense when it comes to repetition and perhaps a distillation or sublimation of the quintessence of the magician. There's also the symbol of purification included and to rid oneself of deep emotional trauma that purification and repetition would make sense.

The camel mentioned in the description could represent adaptation as well as endurance. The crown often symbolizes the divine, as well as the sun, and the completion of the Great Work as well as the union of opposites, the spiritualization of matter, and harmony among the elements. Whenever you see crowns mentioned throughout the Ars Goetia, keep this in mind.

10: Buer

PRESIDENT

Color: Orange
Incense: Storax
Metal: Mercury
Planet: Mercury
Element: Fire

*The 10th spirit is **Buer**, a great president who appears in Sagittarius that is his shape when the sun is there. He teaches philosophy both moral and natural, and the logical arts, and the virtues of all herbs and plants. He heals all distempers in men and gives good familiars. He governs over 50 Legions of spirits.*

The Alchemical Breakdown:

Some of these seals are rather complex, including that of this particular demonic force. There is the symbol for liquid mercury, which inside you see a crossbars in the four dots suggesting distilled vinegar, combined with iron and silver.

So, while there is the suggestion of distillation of thoughts through radical action or change or possibly even calcification by burning something to white ash, I'm not quite sure what this process is. It probably could be a recipe to make silver amalgam. The process is to file iron into a fine powder and place it in a glass vessel. Add to that liquid mercury. Seal the vessel and bury it for seven days. When you remove it, wash it with water and this creates silver amalgam, which is a mixture of iron and mercury.

Symbolically, this could suggest ideas (mercury) grounded in reality (earth and iron).

Perhaps you will look at it and be able to see something more. But looking at all of these symbolic components individually, it suggests there's more to Buer than his initial description of teaching herbalism and herbal medicine, healing emotional discord, giving good familiars, and teaching philosophy and logic. Clearly this demon is very mercurial, but also very practical. This could suggest, all of these symbols combined, that the distillation of our thought patterns can bring more focus and clarity leading to tangible results.

11: Gusion

DUKE

Color: Green
Incense: Sandalwood
Metal: Copper
Planet: Venus
Element: Water

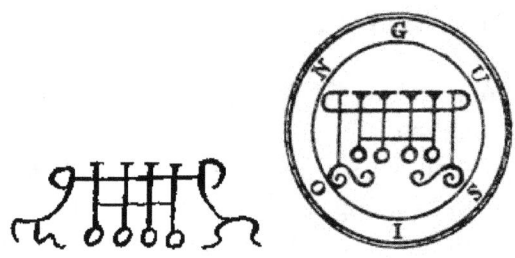

The 11th spirit is a great and strong duke called **Gusoin/Gusion.** *He appears like a xenophilus and he tells of all things past, present and to come. He shows the meaning of all questions you can ask, and he reconciles friends and gives honor and dignity to any. He rules over 40 legions of spirits.*

The Alchemical Breakdown:

Included in the seal of Gusion are symbols for water, day, venus/copper, solidification, silver and the moon (this is important), and binding. It appears to be a recipe to create silver from copper. A recipe for making silver from copper can be found in the medieval collection of alchemical recipes known as the *Mappae Clavicula*. It says: "Take verdigris, which is a green pigment made from copper, and grind it with salt and vinegar. Then put it in a clay pot and cover it with another pot. Lute them well and place them in a furnace. Heat them until the verdigris becomes red. Then take it out and wash it with water. You will have fine silver."

The description "he appears like a xenophilus" means a lover of different cultures, suggesting an open-mindedness and a willingness to learn, as well as being accepting of others. The process of "binding" one substance to another makes sense in the scope that Gusion can reconcile and conciliate friendships and bring one honor and dignity. This Daemonic force also brings with it a psychic ability (hence the symbol for silver) that suggests this is a good Daemon to work with for Divination as well, which is also mentioned in the description with "he tells of all things past, present, and to come."

12: Sitri

PRINCE

Color: Blue
Incense: Cedar
Metal: Tin
Planet: Jupiter
Element: Earth
(Also Syrty)

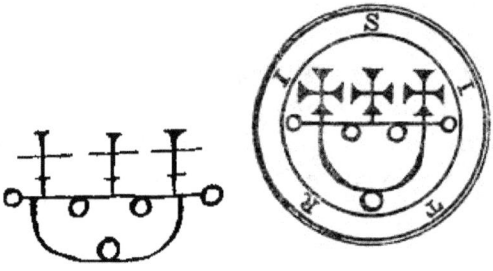

The 12th spirit is **Sitri.** *He is a great prince and appears at first with a leopard's face, and wings as a griffin. But afterwards at the command of the exorcist, he puts on a human shape very beautiful, inflaming men with women's love, and women with men's love, and causes them to show themselves naked, if it is desired. He governs 60 legions of spirits.*

The Alchemical Breakdown:

What I find most interesting about Sitri is that (s)he is often referred to as a Daemon of sexuality in the feminine by many modern practitioners, but I feel like there is definitely a male/female balance to the sigil as it appears both phallic and womb-like. The alchemical symbols contained in this seal include the symbol for crucible, acid/vinegar, oil, borax or arsenic, and aqua vitae – the water of life. As borax is heated to a high temperature, it loses water and expands into a white mass, which melts to create a clear glassy solid known as borax glass or borax bead with further heating. Perhaps an apt metaphor for lustful feelings solidifying into sexual acts. The water of life perhaps analogous with semen, or the act of sex to reproduce offspring. Liquid to solid. The semen and the egg combine to make flesh.

The leopard represents the element of fire and the power of transformation and regeneration. Leopards are also a symbol of the unconscious mind and its ability to manifest desires. The griffin wings represent sublimation, transforming a solid into a gas or vapor.

13: Beleth

KING

Color: Yellow
Incense: Frankincense
Metal: Gold
Planet: Sun
Element: Earth
(Also Bileth)

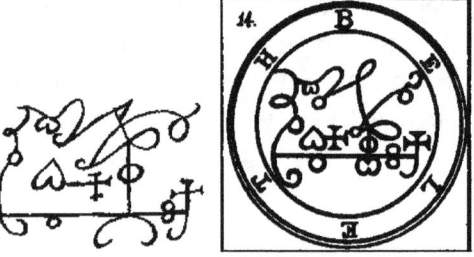

The 13th spirit is called **Beleth.** *He is a mighty king and terrible, riding on a pale horse with trumpets and all other kinds of musical instruments playing before him. He is very furious at his first appearance; that is while the exorcist allay his Courage, for to do that, he must hold a hazel stick in his hand, stretched forth towards the South and East quarters making a triangle without the circle, commanding him into it by the virtue of the bonds and chains of spirits hereafter following. If he does not come into the triangle by your threats, rehearse the bonds and chains before him, and then he will yield obedience and come into it and do what he is commanded by the exorcist. Thet he must receive him courteously, because he is a great king and do homage to him, as the kings and princes do that attend him, and you must have always a silver ring on the middle finger of the left hand, held against your face as they do for Amaimon.*

This king Beleth causes all the love that possibly may be, both of men and women till the master exorcist has had his mind fulfilled. He is of the order of Powers and governs 85 legions of spirits.

The Alchemical Breakdown:

The sigil of Beleth is definitely a recipe because the top squiggly bit is actually the symbol for ½ ounce of gold. There is also the symbol for potassium nitrate which is more pronounced in the left seal, and marcasite – fool's gold. This is clearly a recipe as a preliminary step to create the philosopher's stone, or an experiment in using nitric acid to make aqua regia, a mixture of nitric and hydrochloric acids that can dissolve gold. Now, let's look at these processes in relation to the material.

There is the symbolism of the horse – an animal that represents all the elements, along with power and endurance. The description reminds me of the process of conjuring inner power and eliciting obedience from the shadow-self. Conversely, it could be a recipe for dissolution of the ego. Perhaps both as each process – one manifesting, one dissolving – can bring or dissolve "love" (i.e. Gold) at the will of the magician. Beleth is also one of the Ars Goetia's many "Death Daemonic" and is often invoked to bring comfort and love to those who are grieving. Many believe the hazel wand is for exorcising and banishing spirits – it can be – because hazel is also the tree associated with love and healing. When working necromancy with Beleth, the hazel wand aids in divination to speak with the dead to bring love and healing to the living who are grieving. So if you're using this wand to banish – it's to banish grief.

14: Leraje

MARQUIS

Color: Violet
Incense: Jasmine
Metal: Silver
Planet: Moon
Element: Fire

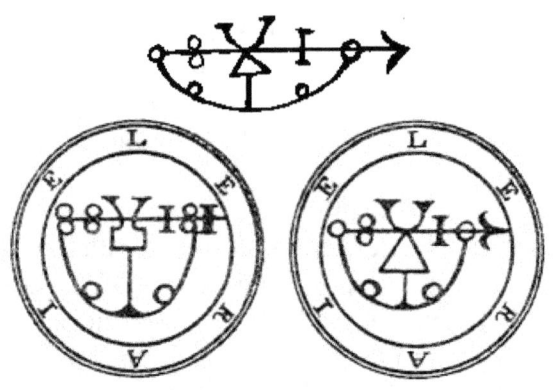

*The 14th spirit is called **Lerathe** (or Leraje). He is a Marquis great in power showing himself in the likeness of an archer, clad in green carrying a bow and quiver. He causes all great battles and contests and causes the wounds to putrefy that are made with arrows by archers this belong to Sagittarius. He governs 30 legions of spirits.*

The Alchemical Breakdown:

Leraje's seal appears to describe a process of purification of matter via fire. Symbols of marcasite (fool's gold, bismuth, fire stone), fire, purification, and the crucible are all present in this seal. Perhaps this is why so many spirits of the Ars Goetia are considered "demonic" in the sense that they are malevolent. Because sometimes you have to break a substance down to purify it and transform it into something more desirable. Sometimes we have to destroy the life we have to build a better one. The inclination for the spirits of Ars Goetia to purify and break down the mental, emotional and physical may seem malevolent to those who perceive drastic change as "bad", but ultimately, it's for the magician's or alchemist's own good. Which is why if we're going to call these spirits "demons" I prefer we call them daemons or daimons (the words demon comes from) – divine intelligences, replete with wisdom.

The symbolism of the archer suggests being direct, on point, shooting for something, and ambition. He causes great battles and contests and causes wounds to putrefy. In the context of this description, with some attributes listed for both fire AND water, it suggests that Leraje can be worked with to both send and remove psychic/emotional attacks. Remember, that if a Daemon is good at one thing – it's often good at the opposite, too, and the varying degrees between. Purifying through fire is a rather violent process. Much like how the phoenix bursts into flame and is reduced to ash. But from that ash can come rebirth anew.

15: Eligos

DUKE

Color: Green
Incense: Sandalwood
Metal: Copper
Planet: Venus
Element: Water
(Also Eligor)

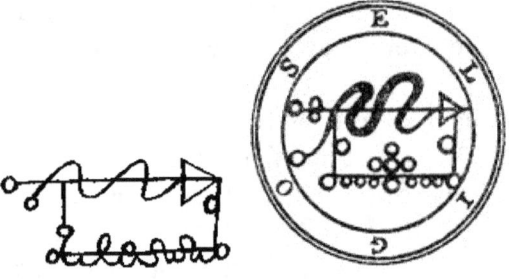

The 15th spirit is called **Eligor**. *A great duke, he appears in the form of a goodly knight carrying a lance, an insignia and a serpent. He discovers hidden things and knows things to come, and of wars and how the soldiers will and shall meet. He causes the love of lords and great persons. He governs 60 legions of spirits.*

The Alchemical Breakdown:

Within this seal are symbols suggesting a process that includes calcination to dissolution. Calcination is the process of heating a substance to a high temperature, and turning it into ash, while dissolution is the process of dissolving a substance in a solvent, such as water.

While both are among the various steps of alchemy, calcination comes before dissolution. Psychologically, calcination in this case represents the burning away of attachments, while dissolution represents the breaking down of psychological barriers and defenses.

The symbols contained in the seal include the serpent and arrow (lance) which represent the shedding of skin and transformation of the self, the symbol of aqua vitae (water of life), calx (the powder or ash formed by calcination) and quicklime or calcium oxide formed by roasting limestone. In context of the description, this appears to be a recipe for shadow work. Burning away attachments and ideas/things that no longer serve you, and removing barriers like defensive behaviors or thoughts that could be holding one back.

16: Zepar

DUKE

Color: Green
Incense: Sandalwood
Metal: Copper
Planet: Venus
Element: Earth

*The 16th spirit is called **Zepar**. He is a great duke and appears in red apparel and is armed like a soldier. His office is to cause women to love men and to bring them together in love. He also makes them barren. He governs 26 legions of inferior spirits.*

The Alchemical Breakdown:

Within the seal of Zepar are symbols for calcination, incineration/ash, the sun and the aurum potable, which is a drinkable alchemical preparation of gold, to which calcination is necessary to prepare. I can also see symbols for summer (perhaps the time at which the operation should be performed), vinegar made from wine (the souring of love, or even the bite of it), copper, and Venus in this seal.

This seal does, in fact, appear to be a recipe to create the second part of the aurum potable, the *Spirit of Gold*. One recipe for the spirit of gold gives these instructions: You would dissolve the gold in distilled vinegar and filter the resulting solution. Then, you heat the preparation made from burnt copper (copper oxide) along with the rock salt (sodium chloride) until a red powder is formed. This becomes the Vitriol of Venus. Next, you'd mix the gold solution with the vitriol of Venus, distill the mixture several times (at least twice it looks like according to the seal), until you obtain a clear liquid. This liquid becomes the *Spirit of Gold*. The spirit of gold is then mixed with the spirit of silver (see Berith) and heated gently for 40 days to create the aurum potable.

In the description of Zepar, we notice the color red (*Vitriol of Venus*), and the purpose to cause women and men to love one another, to bring them together, and to cause them to be barren/infertile. Remember that red is the color of the third stage of the alchemical work and signifies the completion and perfection of matter, the union of opposites (male and female perhaps), and the creation of the philosopher's stone, the ultimate goal of alchemy. It is associated with the element of fire, the planet (celestial body) Sol (the sun), and the metal gold.

There is a lot of gold and solar imagery in both the description and the seal. Many books list Zepar with the celestial correspondence of Venus (due to the love in the description), and copper instead of gold. And while the symbols within the sigil do give a nod toward copper and Venus, they are definitely more solar. You might say that Zepar is the fire part of earth or vice versa. Which makes sense when we're talking about calcination. If calcination burns away impurities and attachments, perhaps enhancing love as a result – then it stands to reason that calcination could also be destructive toward "attachments" like love interests generally. And perhaps that's where "he also makes them barren" comes in. Again, it's always good to keep in mind the dualistic and "shades of gray" of every Daemonic force.

17: Botis

PRESIDENT

Color: Orange
Incense: Storax
Metal: Mercury
Planet: Mercury
Element: Water

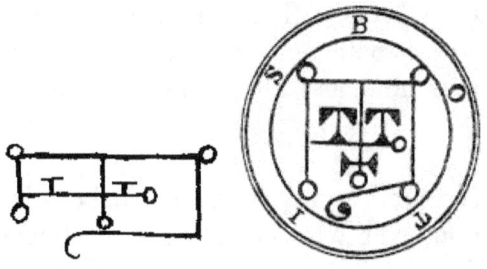

The 17th spirit is called **Botis.** *A great president and an earl; he appears at first in the form of an ugly viper. Then, at the command of the magician he puts on human shape, with great teeth, two horns, carrying a sharp bright sword in his hand. He tells of all things past and to come and reconciles friends and foes. He governs 60 legions of spirits*

The Alchemical Breakdown:

There are symbols here for mercury and sublimation. With a low melting point, it easily sublimates when heated. Sublimation is a process where a solid substance turns into a gas, without going through a liquid state. Which is interesting since Botis is listed as a Daemonic force with the element water. There are symbols present for the gold solution (arum potable, which can be consumed), and distilled vinegar. Also, a symbol for alum or clay for the container in which to put this alchemical mixture.

While Botis is listed as a spirit ruled by water, there are very airy qualities here (as makes sense with mercury). A melding of the emotional and mental. The thinking and the feeling aspects of the magician.

One possible alchemical recipe that includes the ingredients based on the symbols in the seal is the preparation of the philosopher's mercury. The philosopher's mercury was believed to be a pure and volatile form of mercury that could dissolve gold and silver and form amalgams with them.

In the description, the viper, or snake, denotes self-transformation, even wisdom. The sword imagery suggests quick decision making or a sharp mind. Communication in the sharing of emotions with honesty and practicality fits Botis. Clear, concise, wise, and emotionally intelligent/mature communication at that. This, of course, does give one the power to see things for what they are, and to reconcile misunderstandings between people.

18: Bathin

DUKE

Color: Green
Incense: Sandalwood
Metal: Copper
Planet: Venus
Element: Earth

*The 18th spirit is called **Bathin**. He is a mighty and strong duke and appears like a strong man with a tail of a serpent, sitting on a pale colored horse. He knows the virtue of herbs and precious stones and can transport men suddenly from one Country into another. He rules over 30 legions of spirits.*

The Alchemical Breakdown:

The symbols included in the seal consist of day and night (x2), borax, vinegar, crucible (clay), purification, a distillation apparatus, distillation, the patina on copper (verdigris), the moon and silver. It appears to me to be a process of purification via distillation to manifestation.

It also appears to be a recipe for a neutral Borax + Vinegar solution for disinfecting, cleaning, and removing mold and mildew. ½ cup Borax to 1 Gallon of undiluted Vinegar is all you need for that. I would almost expect Bathin to be a Daemon of healing sickness and killing germs.

My first thought when reading the description of Bathin in context of the vinegar and Borax mixture, is Bathin is the medieval Mr. Clean on horseback. I'm kidding, of course, but isn't that a great visual? The horse being symbolic of all the elements (foundation), and the serpent being a symbol for wisdom, knowledge, and all the repetitive cycles within life, make Bathin a Daemon of knowledge. Especially that of herbs and precious stones – and teleportation (or astral travel?), apparently. I've always seen Bathin as a "kitchen" witch's Daemon. Or a Daemon that rules over those who practice traditional craft. I shared this information with a friend and her take on this is that Bathin knows the importance of cleanliness when working with herbs and natural things, and how to stay healthy when traveling. That means clean, clean, clean. Twice a day (day and night) for at least two days? Is it a process of purification via distillation (of the vinegar perhaps) to manifestation of that purification (cleanliness)? Or is it analogous to the process of learning? You learn it, you do it, you refine/practice it, you repeat. Perhaps the moon imagery refers to the purification and distillation of the imagination via astral travel or meditation, hence traveling. It's food for thought.

19: Sallos

DUKE

Color: Green
Incense: Sandalwood
Metal: Copper
Planet: Venus
Element: Earth
(Also Saleos)

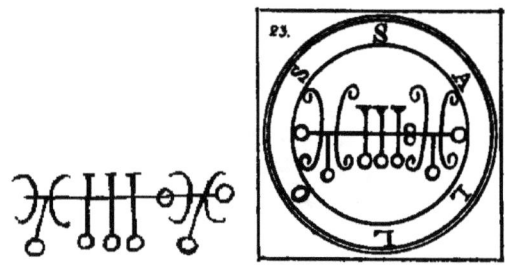

The 19th spirit is called **Saleos**. *He is a great and mighty duke, and appears in the form of a gallant soldier, riding on a Crocodile, with a duke's crown on his head peaceably. He causes the love of women to men and men to women. He governs 30 legions of spirits.*

The Alchemical Breakdown:

If you're noticing how many Daemons rule over friendship, human interaction, and love – you're not wrong. The magicians of old valued relationships with people just as much as we do today, and were likely introverts who longed for love, and solid friendships, etc... I think with

Sallos' appearance, the fact that he rides a crocodile – as a messenger of the gods perhaps? Or perhaps the crocodile, being both an earth and water creature, deals with both physical and emotional relationships. The Egyptian view of the crocodile being a protectorate and a creature representing fertility also comes to mind here. Once again, this Daemon rules over love.

Within the seal we find the symbols for summer, the alchemical preparation of gold, 3 days building layer upon layer, copper, and eventual distillation.

One possible alchemical recipe or process that contains the above ingredients is the projection of the philosopher's stone onto a base metal (copper). Projection is the act of applying a small amount of the philosopher's stone, also called the elixir or the powder, to a molten base metal in order to transmute it into gold or silver.

This does suggest this is a binding operation. Binding gold to copper. Metaphorically binding men to women and women to men, this alchemical process works in the context of the Daemon's purpose. As an alchemical operation within the self, it might suggest an operation to find inner confidence that makes one more attractive to the opposite sex. Or even cleansing and primping the physical body, adorning it with finery, in order to attract the eye of the opposite sex. Sallos is the Goetia's equivalent to the Daemon Rosier in the Dukanté hierarchy and can be invoked during weddings to bind the marriage.

20: Purson

KING

Color: Yellow
Incense: Frankincense
Metal: Gold
Planet: Sun
Element: Earth

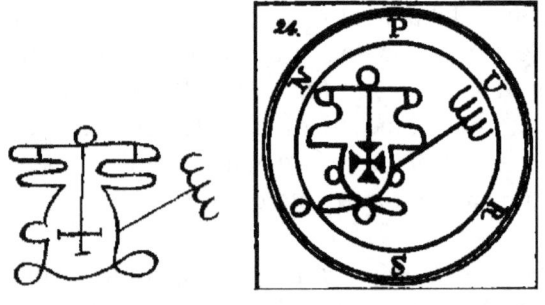

*The 20th spirit is called **Purson**. A great king, he appears commonly like a man with a lion's face, carrying a cruel viper in his hand, and riding on a bear. Going before him are many trumpets sounding. He knows hidden things and can discover treasures and tell all things present past and to come. He can take a body either human or airy, and answer truly of all earthly things, both secret and divine, and of the creation of the world, he brings forth good familiars. Under his government are 22 legions of spirits, partly of the order of virtues and partly of the order of thrones.*

The Alchemical Breakdown:

The seal of Purson includes the symbol of calcination (twice) and alumen, as well as the symbols for salt, the sun and the earth. It sounds very much like a recipe for alum, a salt substance that is used in medicines, tanning leather, dying cloth, and fireproofing. The latter use for Purson might suggest protection of some sort. Or it could simply be suggesting that the first step to finding wisdom (Gold) is to calcinate the matter into a salt. As in, the first step to solving a problem is admitting there is a problem.

Visually, the seal looks like a little guy carrying a pitchfork, or a creature with a barbed tail. But let's look at what we have additionally. We have the color yellow (associated with all the Kings) which again, represents the maturation and ripening of matter, the illumination of the mind, and the preparation for the final stages of the great work. Lions, snakes, and bears are mentioned in the description, and some liken the seal to a lion. If we interpret these things alchemically in conjunction with the description of the spirit, it appears that this seal represents transformation of the self as an eternal process for ascension and enlightenment. This accounts for the spirit being worked with to find treasure and hidden things and to know the past and future.

Calcination is also a process of transformation by breaking down a substance through the application of heat. Substance – earth, heat – fire. The end result being ascension and enlightenment. When we break down the whole into its parts, we can see things more clearly.

21: Marax

PRESIDENT/EARL

Color: Orange
Incense: Storax
Metal: Mercury
Planet: Mercury
Element: Earth

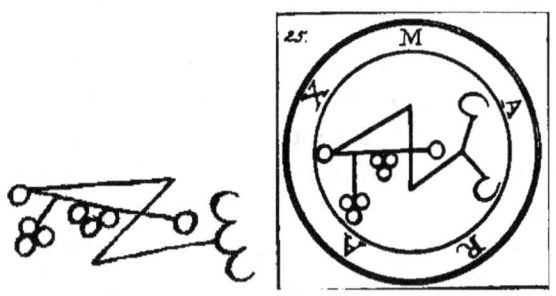

*The 21st spirit is called **Morax**. He is a great earl and a president. He appears like a great bull with a man's face, His office is to make men very knowing in astronomy, and all the other Liberal sciences; he can give good familiars and is very wise. He knows the virtues of herbs and precious stones. He governs 30 legions of spirits.*

The Alchemical Breakdown:

In this seal we see the symbol for the Mercury of Saturn (red lead). When red lead is heated in a current of air, it appears as liquid mercury. Lead corresponds with earth. There are also the symbols of binding, calcination, and distilled vinegar. Some thoughts I had about this is that it is a mercurial binding to earth – the knowledge of tangible things that are of the natural world. Including herbs and stones as mentioned in the spirit's description.

The Bull is very symbolic of earth, and the purification of matter by fire so that matter can transform or ascend to something higher. There is a lot going on here. You'll notice in the description that it seems Marax has knowledge of earthly things but is also transcendent and wise in the ways of the universe and other liberal sciences. The liberal sciences cover subjects such as literature, history, languages, philosophy, mathematics, and natural sciences. So, Marax, it stands to reason, is a spirit that can hasten the spiritual alchemical process within the magician leading to greater knowledge of the physical world and can transform (enlighten) the mind of the magician through that knowledge.

22: Ipos

PRINCE/EARL

Color: Blue
Incense: Cedar
Metal: Tin
Planet: Jupiter
Element: Water

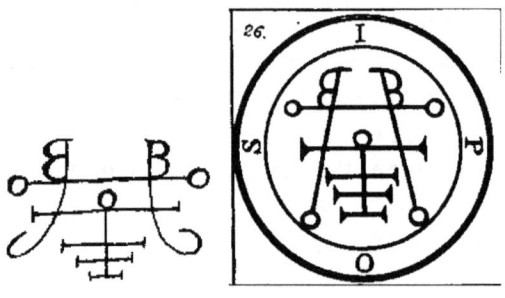

*The 22ⁿᵈ spirit is called **Ipos**. He is an earl and a mighty prince, and appears in the form of an angel, with a lion's head, goose's feet, and a hare's tail. He knows things past and to come and he makes men witty and bold. He governs 36 legions of spirits,*

The Alchemical Breakdown:

This particular seal seems to show the process of smelting chemical arsenic with tin. In the process of smelting, combined with copper, this arsenic and tin would make bronze, and produce a stronger final product. The symbols for Tin and Jupiter, arsenic, and copper/brass are here.

The description of the spirit is rather detailed. The angel with a lion's head, goose feet, and a hare's tail suggests a creature that brings messages from the divine to enlighten the magician. I also liken the animal combination to the process of smelting. The arsenic and tin were brought together by heat and added to copper, creating bronze. Tempering the metal through heating, and then cooling it with water changes its physical nature into something harder.

If you really think about this, many spirits of the Goetia are considered "evil" or "malevolent" to those with a Judeo-Christian mindset, and Ipos comes to mind here because most of these spirits will bring knowledge, but sometimes in hard earned lessons that feel negative and cruel, but ultimately make the magician or alchemist stronger. Nature is both cruel and kind, and that could be said for both the spirits of Ars Goetia, and the process of alchemy.

23: Aim

DUKE

Color: Green
Incense: Sandalwood
Metal: Copper
Planet: Venus
Element: Fire

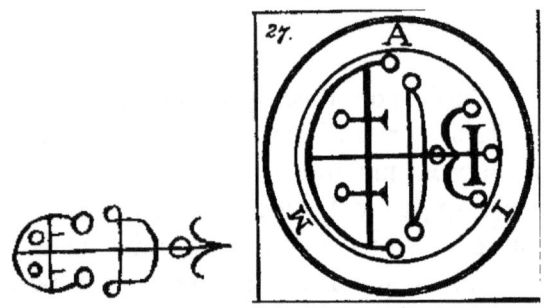

*The 23^d spirit is called **Aim**. He is a great duke and strong. He appears in the form of a very handsome man in body, but with 3 heads. The first like a serpent, the second like a man with 2 stars in his forehead, the third is like a cat. He rides on a viper, carrying a fire brand in his hand burning, wherewith he sets cities, castles, and great places on fire. He makes one witty in all manner of ways and gives true answers to private matters. He governs 26 legions of infernal spirits.*

The Alchemical Breakdown:

The first thing you're going to notice is that there are two different sigils for Aim. Aim with the arrow pointing right, and Aim with no arrow, but instead what appears to be a bow and a vertical line with a circle to the right at that vertical line's center. The latter is the more common sigil that we often see when we look up this seal in an image search. The one with the arrow is from the Sloane manuscript 3825. I almost feel like this might have been an attempted correction because the left sigil suggests iron sulphate, when it should have been copper sulphate. That said - that interpretation may have been misguided.

The seal of Aim appears to be a formula for making glass. You can see the symbols for white arsenic, copper/Venus, antimony prepared spagyrically, glass, alumen, salt (matter), and white clay (as a vessel), As well as the symbol for incineration. It's also highly possible the newer seal has the symbol for ash. The symbol for antimony is also the symbol of glass of antimony. Created by grinding crude antimony and calcinating it (via incineration) in an earthen crucible (clay), it was vitrified in a wind furnace, stirred with an iron rod, and then became translucent with a red/yellow color. That said, it does dissolve in any acidic fluid, One can make an acidic fluid with a preparation of arsenic in water. What can this preparation tell us about Aim? Several things. First, Aim gives perspective and inspiration through that different perspective. When we look through a yellow-orange glass, the world looks different. Glass can create reflection and can change how we see light. It can change how we see our situation, ourselves, and the world around us.

There's still more to unpack here, though. Aim is also said to appear with three heads. The first, a serpent – the wisdom and cyclical nature of the alchemical work. The second, a man with two stars upon his forehead – the mundane, representing man on earth but still connected to all that is. Third, a cat – symbolizing the energy of transformation and hidden knowledge. He rides a viper (another snake) – again representing wisdom and the never-ending cycles of life, death, and rebirth. He carries a fire brand, which I always view as a way to communicate that Aim is an active force of energy, always moving and spurring things forward.

All of this, together, still suggests, to me, the inner alchemical work of transforming our inner narratives and perspectives to change the world around us. We're making a looking glass to see the world in a new light that is active and forward moving.

24: Naberius

MARQUIS

Color: Violet
Incense: Jasmine
Metal: Silver
Planet: Moon
Element: Air

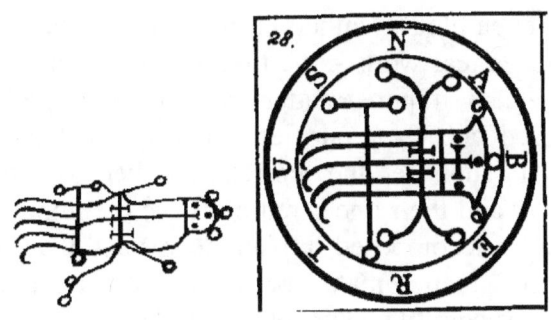

*The 24th spirit is called **Naberius**. He is a most valiant marquis, and appears in the form of a black crow, fluttering about the circle. When he speaks, it is with a hoarse voice. He makes men cunning in all arts and sciences, but especially in the art of rhetoric. He restores lost dignity and honors, and he governs 19 Legions of spirits.*

The Alchemical Breakdown:

In this seal we see the symbol for oil of vitriol, sulfuric acid, which could also be seen as a symbol for salt – an acid and alkali base? It could also be faux gold as well. There is also the alchemical symbol for sulfur (that capital

T with the circles at the end of each horizontal line and the bottom of the vertical line), the symbol for nitrum commune – potassium nitrate, often made from the decay of animal waste. There are also symbols for the moon and silver in this seal, and white arsenic, the latter being common in various Daemonic seals. From what I can gather from this, it could be a recipe of how to gild other metals or objects with silver. Which makes me think that it is quite possible, Naberius could be worked with in glamour magick.

The mention of a black crow (as some crows can have gray, white, or even bluish feathers) is symbolic of the first stage of the alchemical work – the blackening and putrefaction. This is where impure matter (animal dung perhaps) is decomposed and then purified. In a spiritual alchemical process, I suppose the correlation here is that the practitioner and their undesired traits are the impure matter that must be decomposed (broken down) and then purified. The phrase, practice makes perfect (or at least as close to perfection as possible, I suppose) would apply.

25: Glasya-Labolas

PRESIDENT

Color: Orange
Incense: Storax
Metal: Mercury
Planet: Mercury
Element: Fire

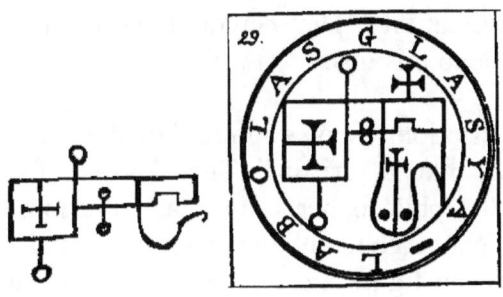

The 25th spirit is called **Glasya Labolas**. *He is a mighty president and shows himself in the form of a dog with wings like a griffin. He teaches all arts in an instant and is an author of bloodshed and manslaughter. He tells all things past and to come if desired and causes love of friends and foes. He can make a man go invisible, and he has under his rule 36 legions of spirits.*

The Alchemical Breakdown:

This sigil is rather interesting in that it contains symbols for Mercury, day and night, gold, spirit distillation, distilled vinegar (from sour wine no less), purification, autumn, and filtration. When you add vinegar to biogenic sand, the calcium carbonate produces CO_2. It bubbles as it dissolves. I imagine the process might read something like – distill the vinegar (made of sour wine) to purify it for 24 hours (day and night) and then filter the result through sand. But what could this possibly mean? Immediately what came to mind was the phrase, when you make bad decisions, or decisions you think are good, but go terribly wrong, there is a process to purify the bad (sour) into something beneficial. Like learning from one's mistakes. The "art in an instant" in the description makes me think of bright flashes of insight or inspiration --- divination – perhaps even fire scrying. Or better yet, creativity. The mercurial aspect of this process might allude to this insight as well.

In the description, "shows himself in the form of a dog, with wings like a griffin." The dog is often used to represent the philosopher's stone and the journey of the soul from ignorance to enlightenment. You make a mistake (like causing a fight) and you learn from it. Fuck around and find out, I suppose. Griffins have wings of eagles, and if the dog has wings of an eagle (or griffin), it suggests the soul of the magician will bring them to enlightenment.

Glasya_Labolas could also simply represent the whole of the Great Work. I've always said Daemons are lesson teachers, and in particular, Glasya-Labolas does seem to embody this idea.

26: Bune

DUKE

Color: Green
Incense: Sandalwood
Metal: Copper
Planet: Venus
Element: Earth

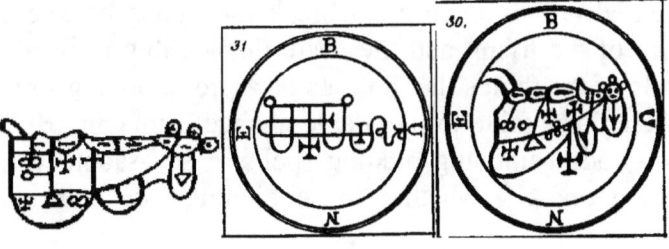

*The 26th spirit is called **Bune**. He is a strong, great, and mighty duke, and appears in the form of a dragon with three heads, one like a dog, and the other like a griffin. The 3d like a man. He speaks with a high and comely voice. He changes the places of the dead and causes those spirits that are under him to gather together upon their sepulchers. He gives riches to a man and makes him wise and eloquent. He gives true answers to your demands and governs 30 legions of spirits.*

The Alchemical Breakdown:

Bune is another of the death Daemonic. In this case, he is often worked with to bring forth the dead for necromancy (speaking or divining with the dead). He brings the dead back to their place of burial. In this seal we have the symbols for oil of vitriol, but could also be the residue after calcination, alumen or potassium aluminium sulphate, calcination, hairy alum, vinegar/acid, fire, white arsenic, purification (could be read as separation, too), common olive oil, a copper vessel, and to dissolve. There is really a lot to unpack here, and I feel as though I've stumbled across a recipe that is rather involved and detailed.

I've summed it up (probably insufficiently) to this: To separate, loosen, or destroy matter through calcination. Potentially, in this case, to break the bonds between the realm of the living and the dead. Or possibly to break the bonds of the things that hold us back from moving forward or being adaptable to inevitable change. I imagine Bune is also good at undoing binding spells or self-sabotage from binding oneself, whether those bindings are spiritual or physical.

In the description we have mention of a dragon, a symbol of sulfur and chaos before order. A symbol of the first matter or raw material. This dragon has three heads: that of a dog, a griffin, and a man. The dog, again, represents the journey of the soul, the griffin the power of transformation, and the man – the balanced union of masculine and feminine and a symbol of the result of the Great Work.

It's interesting because the symbolism, in some cases, feels like it's all over the place but it all comes down to earth. We are of the earth; we go back to the earth in decomposition. But while we're on this physical earth, it is our job to embark on The Great Work, to achieve that balance and to perfect ourselves. The riches Bune brings are likely in wisdom but could also be in a prosperous life. A long life embarking on The Great Work can make a man wise and more eloquent.

27: Ronove

MARQUIS

Color: Violet
Incense: Jasmine
Metal: Silver
Planet: Moon
Element: Air

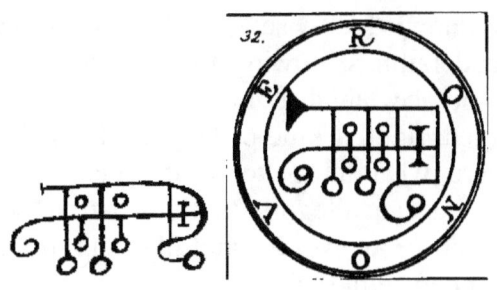

*The 27th spirit is called **Ronove**. He appears in the form of a monster. He teaches the art of rhetoric very well, and gives good servants, knowledge of tongues, and favor of friends and foes. He is a marquis and a great earl, and he commands 19 legions of spirits.*

The Alchemical Breakdown:

In the seal, we see the symbol of silver mixed with mercury, silver again, white arsenic, days (x4), strong water (nitric acid), and distillation (x2 – two days?). After discussing these elements with a friend who understands chemistry, this appears to be a recipe for processing silver. If I understand correctly, mixing silver with mercury creates an amalgam, which is a soft, silver-white alloy. Adding nitric acid to this amalgam causes the mercury to dissolve and form mercury nitrate, leaving behind silver nitrate. White arsenic, or arsenic trioxide, can react with nitric acid to form arsenic acid, which is a strong oxidizing agent. Distilling this mixture can separate the volatile components, such as nitric acid and arsenic acid, from the less volatile ones, such as silver nitrate and mercury nitrate. It is important to note – however - that this process is **very** dangerous, as it can produce toxic fumes and explosive reactions. I don't recommend anyone trying this in their alchemist's lab anytime soon.

I suppose Ronove's seal could be analogous to a warning to use one's knowledge wisely, and to learn from one's mistakes and failings, vowing to do better next time. Of course, if you accidentally blow yourself or your lab up – lesson learned, right? I kind of laughed at this because I'm still not sure what to make of it, but I can definitely appreciate it as an allegory to think before we act and speak, to choose our words carefully, and to learn all we can before doing stupid things.

Ronove, with his monster head, represents all the alchemists' failings, errors, and the danger of the alchemical process. He could also represent fear. On that same token, the monster symbolism in alchemy often represents the potential for improvement and transformation. This is why so many Daemonolaters view Ronove (sometimes Ronwe when we play the name game) as the ultimate "teacher" spirit.

I also feel like there's something in here about patience and paying attention to detail, and Ronove is very much **that** spirit, who can help you focus and look at the details. To be patient, and to do it over and over again until you refine your skill and learn how to not blow yourself up.

28: Berith

DUKE

Color: Green
Incense: Sandalwood
Metal: Copper
Planet: Venus
Element: Fire
(Also Beal or Bolfry/Bolfri)

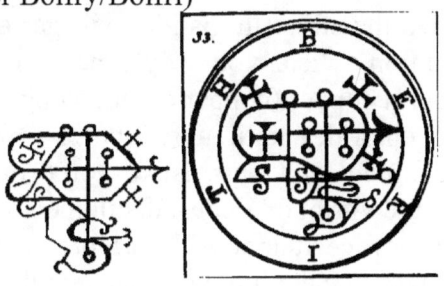

*The 28th spirit in order as Solomon bound them, is named **Berith**. He is a mighty great and terrible duke. He has two other names given to him by men of latter times: **Beal** and **Bolfry**. He appears like a soldier with red clothing, riding on a red horse and a crown of gold upon his head. He gives true answers of things, past present and to come. You must use a ring as is before spoken of Beleth in calling him forth. He can turn all metals into gold. He can give dignity and confirm them to men. He speaks with a very clear and subtle voice. He is a great liar and not to be trusted much. He governs over 26 Legions of spirits.*

The Alchemical Breakdown:

The seal for Berith is a complete recipe in how to make the *Spirit of Silver*, which is the first part of the recipe for the *Arum Potable* – or drinkable gold, which was believed to have mystical and medicinal properties. The seal itself includes the symbols for silver, distilled vinegar, fire, a preparation made from burnt copper, distillation (x2), and rock salt.

According to actual recipes for the spirit of silver, you would dissolve the silver in distilled vinegar and filter the resulting solution. Then, you would heat the preparation made from burnt copper (copper oxide) along with the rock salt (sodium chloride) until a red powder formed. This becomes the *Vitriol of Venus*. Next, you'd mix the silver solution with the vitriol of Venus, distill the mixture several times (at least twice it looks like according to the seal), until you obtain a clear liquid. This liquid becomes the *Spirit of Silver*. To complete your arum potable, you would repeat the same steps using gold instead of silver, and then mix the two resulting spirits together in a glass vessel and seal it. Once this is done, you'd place it in gentle heat for 40 days, and the end result is the aurum potable.

I had to really think about this. There is a great deal of allusion to divination in the recipe just by the nature of its design, and I wonder if the spirit of silver alone might be used to enhance visions, so in turn, Berith could be utilized to help bring visions, too. And his description does clearly suggest this.

The description also paints Berith as a liar, and that could be in the correspondences. Because if you look at those correspondences, the metal is copper and the planet Venus, and the element fire. Yet, there is a great deal of water energy going into the preparation of the spirit of silver. So, with Berith, not all is as it seems. There is a hidden watery undercurrent here that is deceptive to the untrained eye. There are tells here. Like that he can turn **all metals** into **gold**. The recipe basically turns copper oxide and silver into a spirit of silver, which the recipe can be repeated for gold to create the aurum potable.

Allegorically, this is a process of being able to see things clearly and see through the facade, or to turn any situation to your favor by knowing how to proceed. How to fill in the blanks to turn something less lustrous into gold – i.e. wisdom, knowledge, understanding.

The red horse in the description could refer to the vitriol of Venus as the foundation for both halves of the aurum potable. The crown of gold alludes to the final product - the aurum potable itself.

29: Astaroth

DUKE

Color: Green
Incense: Sandalwood
Metal: Copper
Planet: Venus
Element: Earth

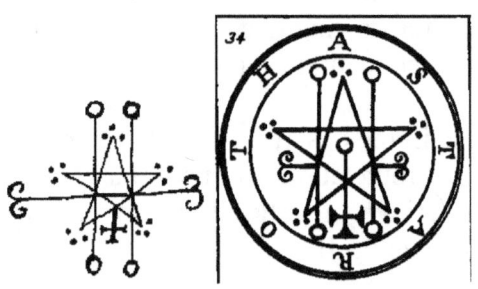

*The 29th spirit in order is named **Astaroth**. He is a Mighty and strong duke and appears in the form of an unbeautiful angel, riding on an infernal dragon, and carrying in his right hand a viper. You must not let him come too near you lest he does you damage by his stinking breath. Therefore, the exorcist must hold the magical ring near to his face and you will defend him. He gives true answers of things present past and to come and can discover all secrets; he will declare willingly how the spirits fell, if desired, and the reason of his own fall. He can make men wonderful knowing in all liberal sciences. He rules 40 legions of spirits.*

The Alchemical Breakdown:

In the seal of Astaroth, we find the symbol for cacanthum, Venus, arsenic, aurum potable, and aqua vitae (the water of life – whiskey and other distilled spirits essentially). This is most likely a recipe for a **VERY DANGEROUS** red elixir. **DO NOT TRY THE FOLLOWING.** One recipe for making a red elixir from calcanthum and arsenic can be found in a 9th-century text called *The Arabic Book of the Composition of Alchemy by Muhammad ibn Umail*. He wrote: "Take calcanthum, which is a blue-green mineral composed of copper sulfate, and grind it with water. Then take arsenic, which is a poisonous metalloid, and sublimate it in a glass vessel, which means to heat it until it turns into a vapor and then condenses into a solid. Then mix the two substances together and put them in a glass vessel. Seal the vessel and bury it in dung for forty days. Then take it out and heat it gently until the calcanthum and the arsenic are united. This is the red elixir of calcanthum and arsenic, which has the power to transmute metals." Likely poisoning the alchemist in the process.

It is similar enough in ingredients, except the recipe described in the seal seems to have its own flair. Different alchemists had their own recipes for various elixirs and such. The three dots at each point of the pentagram are symbolic of the water of life (aqua vitae). So perhaps this is a different preparation for the beginning process of creating the spirit of silver or the spirit of gold in the preparation of the aurum potable? If so, the arsenic would still be potent because distillation and sublimation do not decrease the potency of a toxic substance like arsenic. But I suspect this preparation, while perhaps meant to transmute metals, **was not meant to be taken internally** or literally! Read on to find out why.

Please note that while the pentagram symbolizes the five classical elements (earth, air, fire, water, and spirit), it also symbolizes calcanthum (copper sulphate or copper oxide depending on the text you read).

Now let's look at the description. I love the warning how you must not let him come near you lest he does you damage by his stinking breath. This obviously means that **vapors of arsenic are deadly**.

I suspect the magickal ring is likely a safety device to keep the alchemist from breathing in vaporized arsenic (not an actual ring you'd put on your finger), which is why it's held "near his face."

In the description it also says Astaroth arrives riding a dragon, perhaps symbolizing the alchemical transformation of matter. He also carries a viper. The angel and the viper both symbolize volatile matter, or substances that turn into vapor when heated. Both are representative of the spiritual aspect of the alchemical work – suggesting this may not be a recipe for proper laboratory alchemy at all, but rather a spiritual one. The copper oxide or copper sulphate (calcanthum) in this case would represent the purification and transformation of the toxic arsenic. The arsenic represents the things that poison us spiritually. Things that poison us spiritually could include obsessions, negative self-talk or unhealthy behaviors or thought patterns.

Perhaps the symbols of aurum potable and aqua vitae, both thought to have medicinal properties, were the only "cures" for arsenic poison back then – and were included in the symbolism as a possible antidote. Though I doubt all the whiskey and potable gold in the world would save you from arsenic poisoning. For spiritual alchemy though, the aqua vitae and aurum potable likely symbolize internal transformation and enlightenment, as well as healing. Recognizing and healing ourselves from our spiritual poisons can make us wiser, and quicker to see poison for what it is whether it's within us, within others, or in the natural world.

30: Forneus

MARQUIS

Color: Violet
Incense: Jasmine
Metal: Silver
Planet: Moon
Element: Water

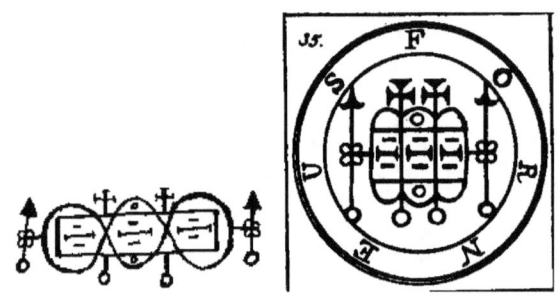

*The 30th spirit is called **Forneus**. He is a mighty great marquis, and appears in the form of a great sea monster. He teaches and makes men wonderfully knowing in the art of rhetoric. He causes men to have a good name, and to have the understanding of tongues. He makes men to be beloved of their foes as well as they be by their friends, and he governs 29 legions of spirits, partly of the order of thrones and partly of angels.*

The Alchemical Breakdown:

This seal contains the symbols for iron x 2, antimony or possibly potable gold, alumen, zinc sulphate (white vitriol), and the hour symbol x 2. There are two possible recipes this could refer to.

The first recipe that contains some of these elements is to make steel from iron by heating it with alumen and water. But this recipe excludes the zinc sulphate. The second a recipe to make aqua regia, which is a powerful solvent that can dissolve gold, by mixing iron, zinc sulphate, and water. This recipe includes no alumen. That said – the symbol for alumen is also the symbol for aurum, or the sun. Despite Forneus' correspondences, no symbols for silver or the moon appear in this seal, making me think that all the watery symbolism suggests how very wet the process, or the final result is. Aqua regia cannot dissolve silver. It's not acidic enough. Reading this in context with the Daemonic force, I am inclined to believe this may be a recipe to make steel from iron, because the symbolism of zinc sulphate (a rather subtle rectangle) could have merely been a stylistic choice of the artist, to potentially throw things off, or to add the iron/mars symbolism into neat little boxes.

You may look at this seal, compare it to 30+ pages of alchemical symbols and see something different.

Now, when looking at the description, the only thing it tells us is that Forneus appears in the form of a giant sea monster. This is perhaps a metaphor for men's churning emotions, which suggests Forneus can teach us to think before acting on emotion, or learning to contain our emotion in favor of rational thinking and carefully considered reactions.

31: Foras

PRESIDENT

Color: Orange
Incense: Storax
Metal: Mercury
Planet: Mercury
Element: Earth

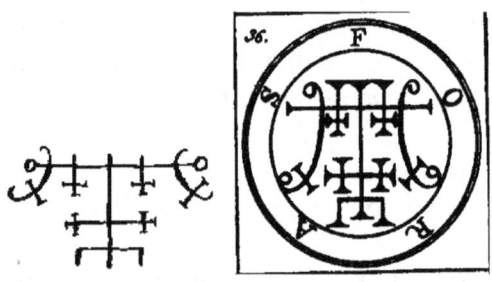

*The 31st spirit in order is named **Foras**. He is a mighty great president and appears in the form of a strong man, in human shape. He can give the understanding to men how they may know the virtues of all herbs and precious stones and teaches them the art of logic and ethics in all their parts if desired. He makes men invisible, witty, eloquent and to live long. He can discover treasures and recover things lost. He rules over 29 legions of spirits.*

The Alchemical Breakdown:

The nature of alchemical symbolism is it can be slightly different from alchemist to alchemist, or a symbol can be darn close to another one. In some cases, symbols can look very much the same. In the case of Foras, we have the symbol for zinc extracted from soot (essence), vinegar, red arsenic and/or the symbol for dissolve. These ingredients, believe it or not, are often employed in recipes that describe the making of philosophical mercury.

Philosophical mercury was also called the elixir of life, as it was supposed to grant immortality and rejuvenation. Philosophical mercury was not the same as ordinary mercury, but rather a secret and elusive product of various alchemical processes. So, this definitely fits with Foras' mercurial correspondences.

The fact that this spirit allegedly appears as a man is what gives Foras the element earth. As mercury is usually associated with air, and all the qualities that go with this including understanding, communication, and enlightenment, and earth is the element of the physical, tangible world, Foras' correspondences in the description makes absolute sense. The man who thinks, understands, and can communicate.

In this case, the process of making the philosophical mercury, is the process of transforming the alchemist into one who thinks, understands, and who can communicate.

32: Asmoday

KING

Color: Yellow
Incense: Frankincense
Metal: Gold
Planet: Sun
Element: Air

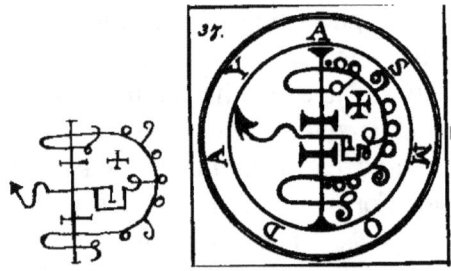

*The 32^d spirit in order is called **Asmoday**. He is a great king, strong and powerful. He appears with 3 heads, whereof the first is like a bull, the second like a man, and the third like a ram. He appears also with a serpent's tail, belching or vomiting up flames of fire out of his mouth. His feet are webbed like a goose, and he sits upon an infernal dragon carrying a lance and a flag in his hands. He is the first and chiefest under the power of **Amaymon**, and goes before all others. When the exorcist has a mind to call him, let it be abroad, and let him stand on his feet all the time of action, with his cap off, for if it be on, Amaymon will deceive him, and cause all his doing to be bewrathed, But as soon as the exorcist sees Asmoday in the shape aforesaid, he shall call him by his name, saying, thou art Asmoday, and he will not deny it; and by and by he will bow down to the ground and he gives the ring of virtues. He teaches the art of arithmetic, geometry, astronomy, and*

all handicrafts absolutely. He gives full and true answers to your demands, and he makes a man invisible. He shows the place where treasures lay, and guards it if it be among the legions of Amaymon. He governs 72 legions of inferior spirits.

The Alchemical Breakdown:

Asmoday appears to potentially be a recipe for making white lead to make paint or cosmetics. The symbols found in this seal include the symbol for 'part of' (as a measurement), vinegar from sour red wine, putrefaction, calcination, oil, lead, urine, and sublimation. One such recipe is found in the *Latin Book of Alchemy*, attributed to the Roman philosopher Seneca, is as follows: Putrefy sour red wine in a glass vessel for 40 days, until it becomes vinegar. Calcine lead in a furnace until it turns white and brittle. Dissolve the lead in the vinegar and filter the solution. Boil the solution until it becomes a thick paste. Sublimate the paste in a glass vessel until a white powder is produced.

Now, again, I DO NOT suggest anyone attempt such experiments knowing what we know nowadays about lead poisoning, but it was common back in the day to use white lead as a paint or cosmetic additive, and slowly poison the people using it for said applications. The line in the description that says, "… and he makes a man invisible" could be pertaining to the cosmetic use of white lead, or to use white paint to cover something up. The deception of the spirit is that a white lead paint or cosmetic can cover up blemishes or mistakes, and the fact that it's poison. There is a lot of hidden deception there.

The description of the spirit contains another multi-headed serpent creature with the head of a bull, another of a man, and third like a ram – all creatures of earth and stability. The dragon spewing fire that he rides upon is symbolic of cycles (perhaps of life and death in this instance). He also carries a lance – in alchemy, a symbol of fire and dry heat, and a flag, which in alchemy often signifies air – the element of the spirit, communication, and breath. In the alchemical emblem of The Azoth (a symbol of the vital force of nature or universal solvent), the flags and lances represent the various stages of the alchemical process as well as the union of opposites such as sulfur and mercury, as well as the balance of the active and the passive.

Asmoday must deceive in that white lead "covers" things. There is a whole airy/fire thing going on with Asmoday which gives us his specialization in mathematics, astronomy, and handicrafts (painting included). These are all disciplines used to make things manifest (earth) in the real world – to create something from just an idea (air). So, there's definitely a passion/idea/creativity angle to this spirit, just as there is in the use of white lead in both paint and cosmetics. The fire breathing dragon always reminds me of the creative spark, or the initial idea, put through thought (air), then used to create a thing. Thus, all of his correspondences make complete sense in this regard.

33: Gaap

PRESIDENT/PRINCE

Color: Orange
Incense: Storax
Metal: Mercury
Planet: Mercury
Element: Air

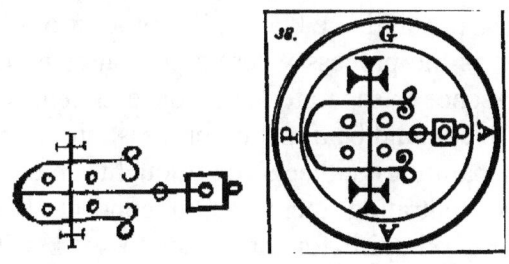

The 33^d spirit is **Gaap**. *He is a great president and a mighty prince. He appears when the sun is in some of the southern signs, In a human shape, going before 4 great and mighty kings, as if he was a guide to conduct them along in their way. His office is to make men knowing in philosophy and all the liberal sciences. He can cause love or hatred and make men insensible. He can teach you how to consecrate those things that belong to the dominion of Amaymon, his king. He can deliver familiars out of the custody of other magicians; and answer truly and perfectly of things past present and to come. He can carry and recarry things most speedily from one kingdom to another, at the will and pleasure of the exorcist. He rules over 66 legions of spirits. He was of the order of potentates.*

The Alchemical Breakdown:

In this sigil we have alchemical symbols for silver and the moon, which accounts for Gaap's abilities for divination. We also have the potential symbol of gum (suggesting binding of some sort), but this symbol could also be for mercury, which would make sense in relation to the correspondences. The alchemical symbols for the sun, quicksilver (mercury), gold leaf (or potentially urine), distillation, salt, and soot or ash are also present.

While I was unable to find any specific recipes that seemed to match Gaap's sigil, we know it's a process of distillation. Distillation is the process where a substance is heated and the pure essence is separated and concentrated. Keeping in mind that this would be a mental process (air and mercury), we are separating subjects or thoughts mentally, and perhaps concentrating them (as in concentration). Gaap might be a good spirit for magicians to work with if they have attention deficit or need to concentrate on a subject for long periods of time. Since part of Gaap's duties, in the description, is to help the querent learn subjects such as philosophy and the liberal sciences, this makes sense.

Gaap is described as appearing in human shape as a guide to Kings. Like many of the Ars Goetia spirits, he can cause love or hatred, can deliver familiars, and see all things. He also has the ability to transport things from one kingdom to another. Astral travel and visualization come to mind here – as those are mental practices. He can muddle one's thoughts or make them clear. Muddle one's communication or make it clear. I suppose that it would be dependent on the intent of the magician as it always is.

34: Furfur

EARL

Color: Red
Incense: Dragon's Blood
Metal: Copper or Silver
Planet: Mars
Element: Fire

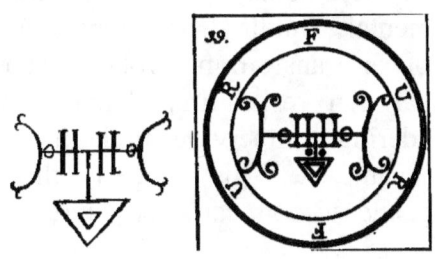

*The 34th spirit is called **Furfur**. He is a great and mighty earl, appearing in the form of an hart (male red deer) with a fiery tail. He never speaks truth, except he be compelled or brought up within a triangle, fire being compelled therein. He will take upon himself the form of an angel being bidden. He speaks with a hoarse voice and will willingly make love between man and wife. He can raise thunder, lightning, blasts, and great tempestuous storms. He gives true answers both of secret and divine things if commanded. He rules over 26 legions of spirits.*

The Alchemical Breakdown:

In this seal we have the symbols for water (possibly aqua vitae), silver, the alchemical preparation of gold, white arsenic, Gemini or fixation x 2 (possibly distillation?), and salt. And even potentially mercury. The water triangle, with the second triangle inside could suggest water within water – or be a symbol for white clay. I couldn't find any exact matches here. Some old alchemical emblems sometimes have inverse symbols (as a design choice or potential inclusion of a blind) and in that case, it could be a symbol for sulfur.

The Gemini symbolism could, potentially, indicate time, such as two hours. You can see how convoluted it can sometimes get. Additionally, it could symbolize fixation, suggesting mental fluidity or communication skills. Fixation involves transforming volatile substances into substances that can resist fire. Fixation stabilizes the substance, rendering it impervious to the flames that would otherwise consume it. This suggests that knowledge, understanding, and wisdom can make on resilient, cunning, and hard to fool or debate.

One possible alchemical recipe the Furfur sigil could trying to convey is a way to use vapors of mercury, salt, and arsenic (via distillation perhaps) to whiten copper to a silvery color. Hence the Copper and Silver correspondences for Furfur. It's definitely a process of transformation. Creating a faux silver from copper --- he never speaks the truth. Fools silver, so to speak.

The fact that Furfur appears as a deer could represent the raw matter, and turns to an angel, volatile matter turned to vapor (the steam of the distillation of salt and arsenic, and possibly mercury turning the copper a silvery color) is symbolic of transformation.

The mention of great storms, thunder, and lightning are all symbolic of fire. It makes me think that the distillation processes for this may have required higher temperatures.

Spiritually, it could mean the desire for transformation needs to be incredibly high. The fact that Fufur gives true answers both secret and divine toward the end of the description (after first saying he never speaks the truth) suggests that this spirit requires the magician to do the inner work to reveal secret and divine knowledge.

35: Marchosias

MARQUIS

Color: Violet
Incense: Jasmine
Metal: Silver
Planet: Moon
Element: Fire

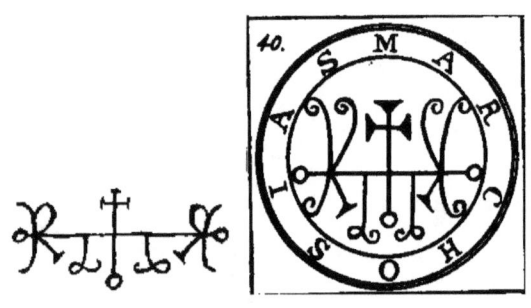

*The 35th spirit is called **Marchosias**. He is a great and mighty marquis appearing at first in the form of a wolf having griffin's wings and a serpent's tail, vomiting up fire out of his mouth. But afterwards, at the command of the exorcist, he puts on the shape of a man, and is a strong fighter. He gives true answers to all questions and is very faithful to the Exorcist in doing his business. He was of the order of dominations and governs 30 legions of spirits. He told his chief master, which was Solomon, that after 1200 years he had hopes to return to the 7th throne.*

The Alchemical Breakdown:

I had two sentences written down in my notes about this seal. The first was, *emotional intelligence and resilience*. The second was, *distillation of the spirit*.

In this seal, you'll find the alchemical symbols for arsenic (or borax), acid/vinegar, day, silver/moon, and spiritus. I suspect it is actually a recipe for a quintessence of silver, though I was unable to find any sample recipes. I also immediately thought it could be a reference to making soap, meaning the symbol for borax might be more appropriate. That said, borax is another dangerous and poisonous substance you wouldn't want to use. Perhaps this recipe was meant to depict, instead, the metaphorical cleansing of the spirit, making Marchosias an ideal spirit to work with if one feels their spirit is tainted somehow.

What's more interesting is the description of Marchosias. This includes a wolf with griffin's wings and a serpent's tail, vomiting fire. It suggests a purification process or the more animalistic or instinctive nature to help one ascend to the higher self. From animal – he turns to a man – who ascends. Whenever a spirit has the moon and silver, we're dealing with a higher intuition and divination. Perhaps a stronger connection to the higher-self.

Some other thoughts – Borax (combined with some type of acid) is sometimes used in soap making as an emulsifier to help blend oil and water-based ingredients. It can increase the cleansing power of soap. When making soap with borax, oils are typically blended with a caustic solution (such as sodium hydroxide) to create a chemical reaction that turns the mixture into soap. In cosmetic products, borax is used as an emulsifier, buffering agent, or preservative in moisturizers, creams, shampoos, gels, lotions, bath bombs, scrubs, and bath salts. Likely in trace amounts. I can't help but really feel like Marchosias is a recipe for body soap or body wash. Whether literal or more hopefully metaphoric.

Now I want to make little Marchosias soaps to cleanse the body and spirit of astral sludge, or to help remove barriers to clearer intuition. Using safer ingredients, of course.

36: Stolas

PRINCE

Color: Blue
Incense: Cedar
Metal: Tin
Planet: Jupiter
Element: Air

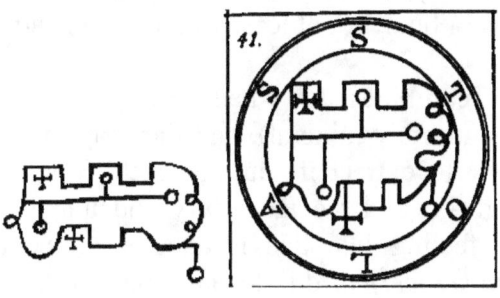

*The 36th spirit is called **Stolas**. He is a great and powerful prince, appearing in the shape of a night raven at first before the exorcist, but afterwards he takes the image of a man. He teaches the art of astronomy, and the virtues of herbs and precious stones. He governs 26 legions of spirits.*

The Alchemical Breakdown:

The Stolas seal describes the process of extracting the quintessence of antimony. Let's first locate the symbols. We have within the emblem the alchemical symbols for day, night, vinegar, salt, and the spagyric preparation of antimony. It's actually a rather simple recipe and I found one in my own alchemy notes from my studies. To extract the quintessence of antimony, take antimony mineral and make a fine powder from it. Then, you would use the best distilled vinegar you could possibly find, or distill it yourself, and put the antimony powder into it. Next, let it stand in a glass container over a gentle heat until the vinegar turns red. At this point you'd remove the red vinegar and set it aside. You'd then repeat the process by adding more distilled vinegar to the antimony and heating until the vinegar turns red again. The fact that we have the symbols for day and night, my guess is you'd repeat the process for 24 hours, or at least all afternoon and evening.

The recipe combines the vinegar (as a solvent), the salt (from the antimony mineral), and the spagyric preparation of antimony to extract its quintessence. Since alchemical practices go beyond the laboratory and into the spiritual, again I'm feeling like this is another recipe that states *practice makes perfect* due to the repetition in the recipe. The quintessence of antimony was often associated with the philosopher's stone, and some alchemists thought it had healing powers. Because of this, it was added to healing elixirs and tinctures for spiritual and emotional well-being and vibrant physical health. It was also thought to awaken higher consciousness and make the mind more receptive. Which could be why learning about the natural world (astronomy, herbs, and stones) is associated with this spirit.

Stolas takes on the form of a raven to start, and then takes on the image of a man. The raven, while often symbolizing death and decay (a transformation from the physical to the spiritual), in this instance may actually represent a transformation of the physical, emotional, and mental, that enriches the spirit and keeps it from death. Hence the power of the quintessence of antimony.

37: Phenex

MARQUIS

Color: Violet
Incense: Jasmine
Metal: Silver
Planet: Moon
Element: Fire

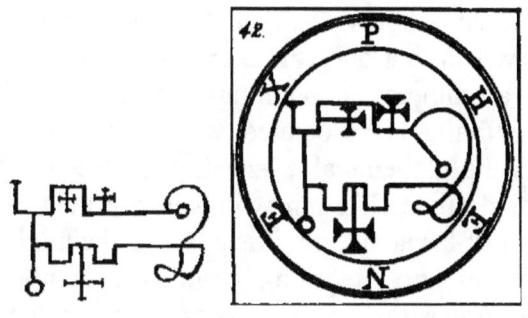

The 37th spirit is called **Phoenix.** He is a great marquis and appears like the bird phoenix having a child's voice. He sings many sweet notes before the exorcist, which he must not regard, but by and by he must bid him put on human shape. Then he will speak marvelously of all wonderful sciences. He is a good and excellent poet and will be willing to do your request. He has hopes to return to the 7th throne after 1200 years more, as he said to Solomon, he governs 20 legions of spirits.

The Alchemical Breakdown:

Included in this seal are the alchemical symbols for day, calcination, fermentation (possibly lutrine or mud of otter), vinegar, and silver. This appears to be another formula to draw out the quintessence of silver. One such recipe suggests beginning by obtaining the calx of gold. This can be achieved using only vinegar, alcohol, or even putrefied urine. The calx of gold is, apparently, a crucial starting point for many alchemical operations. Once you have the calx of gold, you would proceed with distillation. This is to separate and purify the essential components. In a book called *The Book of Quintessence* written by John de Rupescissa, also known as John of Roquetaillade, around 1360, he writes that one can extract the quintessence from stibnite (a mineral containing antimony) using only vinegar. Stibnite is associated with silver, and this step highlights the alchemical connection between calcination, vinegar, and silver. If I am wrong in my interpretation of the symbol of fermentation, it is possible the mud of otter is the probable interpretation because it symbolizes the merging of opposites, or the transformation of matter.

This process immediately suggests to me divination, or enhancing one's psychic ability or intuition to some extent. Transformation of matter is carried through in the mention of the Phoenix, who bursts into flame, turns to ash, and is reborn from those ashes, transformed anew. I am a bit surprised the description for Phenex does not include divination, but he does appear to have a creative aspect, by sparking imagination and inspiration. Or, perhaps, that could be interpreted, in spiritual alchemy, to mean a creative solution to a problem, or just an overall spiritual rebirth and transformation.

38: Halphas

EARL

Color: Red
Incense: Dragon's Blood
Metal: Copper
Planet: Silver
Element: Air (Fire)

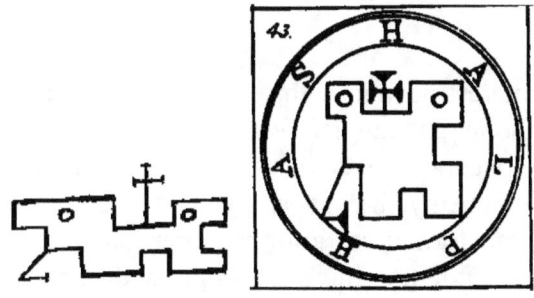

The 38th spirit is called **Halphas.** *He is a great earl and appears in the form of a stock dove and speaks with a hoarse voice. His office is to build up towns and to furnish them with ammunition and weapons, and to send men to war to places appointed. He rules 26 legions of spirits.*

The Alchemical Breakdown:

The symbols in this sigil ran together a bit. Especially the geometric shapes. What I could find was the symbol for orpiment (arsenic trisulfide), alum (or gold), acid/vinegar (or distillation), potentially soot or salt, and calcination. That said, I found an alchemical recipe in my journal that includes all of these things, for a quintessence elixir. First, you'd grind up the orpiment and alum together with a mortar and pestle. Then you'd add the vinegar gradually, stirring clockwise to awaken the essence. Sprinkle in a pinch of salt to represent balance and stability, and then you'd put this in a crucible and subject it to high heat for calcination. As the crucible (your fireproof container) begins to glow an angry red, you would visualize the chaotic essence transforming in the mixture. Then you'd cool your container and collect any residue left behind and store it in a glass vial. It is a symbolic process of finding the hidden gold within. This essence could be used in magick to connect with the higher spiritual self or the divine.

What's interesting about this is while the process seems rather chaotic and angry (with visualizations and such), Halphas appears as a dove – a bird that often represents peace. In alchemy, however, the dove represents the soul and its transformative journey. Spiritually, the process could be about tempering one's anger and rising above it to find the gold within. To grow spiritually and to build an emotional intelligence that helps you build, rather than destroy. Unchecked, anger can lead to war with others.

As with many spirits, I imagine that which can cause calamity can also cause it to subside. With the experience of anger causing us to fight one another, may come the wisdom to grow as a person and avoid similar situations in the future.

39: Malphas

PRESIDENT

Color: Orange
Incense: Storax
Metal: Mercury
Planet: Mercury
Element: Air

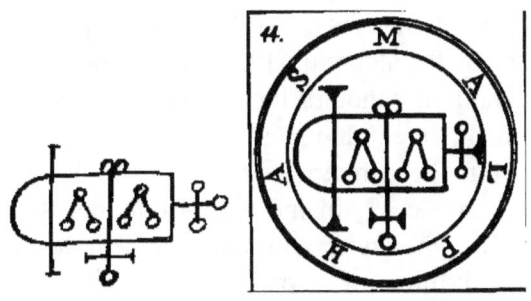

The 39th spirit in order is called **Malphas**. He appears at first in the form like a crow, but afterwards will put on a human shape at the request of the exorcist and speak with a hoarse voice. He is a mighty president and powerful. He can build houses and high towers and he can bring quickly artificers to gather from all places of the world. He can destroy one's enemies, desires, or thoughts, and what they have done. He gives good familiars, and if you make any sacrifices to him, he will receive it kindly and willingly, but he will deceive him who does it. He governs 40 legions of spirits.

The Alchemical Breakdown:

On first glance, Malphas may appear to destroy one's enemies. But how? In the seal we find the symbol for lodestones (x2), metallic mercury, potable gold (possibly antimony), and oil. At first glance, my immediate thought is that this is an operation to attract information. Like placing potable gold between to lodestones somehow equals mercury and knowledge.

While I couldn't find any matching recipes, I then thought that perhaps the symbol of the lodestone was actually a symbol for aqua vitae (water of life), only upside down. It's not unheard of for alchemical symbols to be written upside down, as modern scholars have found inverse alchemical symbols in other emblems. If that were the case, then it may appear to be a recipe for an Aurum Vitae (Gold of Life) that is made by, in individual containers, dissolving gold, metallic mercury, and antimony in aqua regis (a powerful mixture of concentrated nitric acid and hydrochloric acid) and then recombining the liquids to symbolize the union of gold, mercury, and antimony. It was meant to transform the mind, body, and spirit. Alchemists of old may have used it in applications such as healing and for spiritual transformation. Though, frankly, it would not be something one should ingest for obvious reasons.

All of that said, the deception in the seal could be difference between aqua vitae and aqua regis. Clearly, there is a deception in the seal.

In the description, there is a mention of crows, which in alchemy are symbolic of inner workings and gazing into the dark shadow self. They also represent passage and transformation. Spiritually speaking, the process in Malphas' seal may be a recipe to confront the desire to destroy our enemies and those who have hurt us and transform these feelings and desires to something far more productive. Because, as you see, Malphas can also build houses and towers, and can cause people to gather despite their differences. And yet, the raw materials like metallic mercury, and antimony are poison by themselves. Hatred poisons us. The process of Malphas suggests we need to alchemically transform our anger and hatred into something constructive.

40: Raum

EARL

Color: Red
Incense: Dragon's Blood
Metal: Copper or Silver
Planet: Mars
Element: Air (Fire)

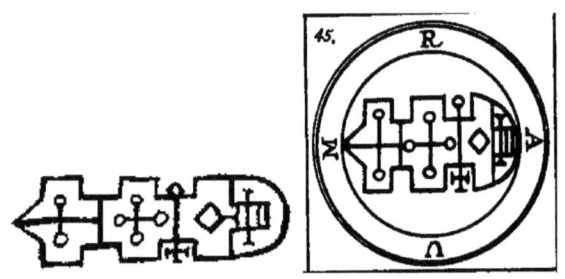

*The 40th spirit is called **Raum**. He is a great earl, and appears at first in the form of a crow but afterwards, at the command of the exorcist he puts on human shape. His office is to steal treasures out of kings houses, and to carry it where he is commanded, and to destroy cities, and the dignities of men. To tell all things past, and what is, and what will be. To cause love between friends and foes. He was of the order of thrones and governs 30 legions of spirits.*

The Alchemical Breakdown:

There is a mental filtration factor to this seal. I wrote about Raum in my journal: *Raum is a hot mess.* I mean that sincerely because his correspondences, according to what is written and what is within the seal, are all over the place. But I can see why this works.

You have the symbol for mercury, which is the air aspect. You have the symbol for antimony, and copper (Venus), and then there's the symbol for filtration. I was unable to find a match for the overall shape of the seal. So, what is going on here? Clearly, mercury represents the mind and the intellect, whereas antimony represents cleansing. Copper represents unity and balance. We have to read these symbols in context with the material – which means the description will better give us an idea what this alchemical recipe is all about in the context of spiritual alchemy.

Much like Malphas, Raum appears as a crow and will then take on human form. Again, the crow is indicative of looking within and facing the shadow self. The correspondences all suggest a watery/fire leaning, which lends well to Raum's divination aspects, as well as love and hate. Raum is about passion, and all of this may suggest this is a process or recipe for taming one's emotions, or to regain control and balance of one's more volatile emotions like lust, hate, and unbridled desire for material possessions.

In the process of Raum, we see this tempering of fiery emotions by cleansing and balancing these darker parts of the self with clear thinking. Filtering out the destructive passionate emotional states (like anger and unbridled desire) to concentrate on those that are productive and useful like love, looking to the future and planning, and learning from mistakes.

41: Focalor

DUKE

Color: Green
Incense: Sandalwood
Metal: Copper
Planet: Venus
Element: Water

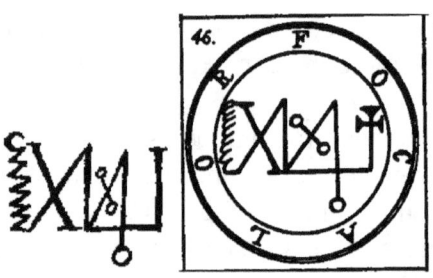

The 41st spirit in order is called **Focalor.** He is a great duke and strong and appears in the form of a man with griffin's wings. His office is to kill men, to drown them in the waters, and to turn over ships of war, for he has power over both winds and seas. But he will not hurt any man or thing, if he be commanded to the contrary by the exorcist. He has hopes to return to the 7th throne after 1000 years. He governs 3 legions of spirits.

The Alchemical Breakdown:

In this seal we find symbols for verdigris (copper acetate), ash (potassium carbonate), vinegar, distillation, and flame. There were a few symbols here that are missing translation since I was unable to find matches. That said, this appears to be a distillation of copper. Copper often represents peace, prosperity, and abundance. This could be why

Focalor is often utilized in modern western magick to stop enemies and gossip as a form of protection. He brings peace.

So why all the destruction of enemies and drowning in the description? I feel this is symbolic imagery, perhaps analogous to the flames and heat, and bubbling of distillation. If anything, perhaps Focalor stops enemies and gossip in its tracks because the spirit uses the energy required to be so hateful (flames), to distill the "matter" into peace (the final distillate). The griffin imagery in the description indicates the union of fire and air, and sublimation (where a solid turns to a gas (thinking) without passing through a liquid (emotion). Almost as if anger and negative attention just dissolves to where there is no emotion left to waste time on harming anyone else. The heated passion of anger and aggression turns to clear thought.

Again, as with all spirits, if one can cause calamity, it can also insulate one from calamity. I was actually expecting a little more from this spirit and sigil, but I think this sums it up rather nicely.

42: Vepar

DUKE

Color: Green
Incense: Sandalwood
Metal: Copper
Planet: Venus
Element: Water

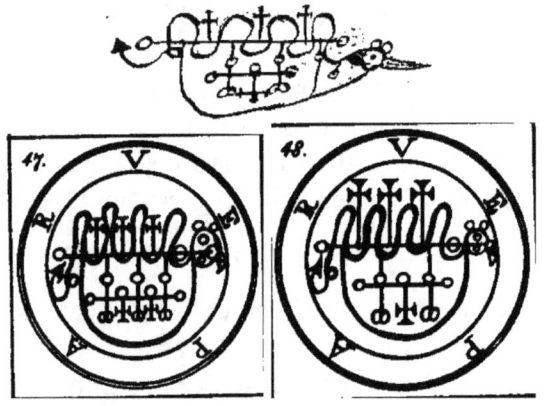

The 42^d spirit is named **Vepar.** *He is a great and strong duke, and appears like a mermaid, his office is to guide the waters, and ships laden with armor thereon he will at the will of the exorcist cause the seas to be rough and stormy, and to appear full of ships. He causes men to die in 3 days with putrefying their sores and wounds, and causing worms in them to breed and he governs 29 legions of spirits.*

The Alchemical Breakdown:

There is really so much here. In the seal we find the symbols for copper, Venus, night, day (possibly 2 days), white arsenic and the symbol for autumn. There is also the serpent symbolism that indicates both water and wisdom.

This seal could actually be a warning (like guiding ships as it were). Remember when I mentioned lab safety? Well, exposing copper to arsenic creates copper arsenite, or Scheele's Green, which, during combination of these elements, creates deadly arsine gas. So, I would read this seal as – if you're going to mix these two things together, be cautious because it could kill you. It could also be suggesting that if you do this, do it in the autumn in the open air and leave it for 2 days before coming back to see what happened?

That said, the spiritual alchemy is less a warning and more of a process of being careful of one's emotions doing spiritual work. The need for balanced emotional states in order to ascend spiritually, perhaps. It could be construed as a warning that extreme emotional turbulence (or stress) is bad for the spirit (and the body). I suppose in this latter interpretation, it would make sense that it's a warning all the way around.

The sigil itself looks like a bird, a swan even – purified matter cleansed and refined. Yet Vepar appears like a mermaid – symbolizing duality and opposing forces to cause transformation of the soul and emotions – both of which are connected in the symbolism of the mermaid. This Vepar mermaid can cause the seas (emotions) to get rough (turbulent) – for the sake of transcendence of the soul as well, it seems.

It is also said in the description that Vepar causes men death in 3 days, causes putrefied sores and wounds, and worms. I'm guessing these could very well be side effects of creating arsine gas.

If Vepar is a warning against accidentally creating arsine gas, it could also be a spiritual warning to not poison yourself with toxic emotional instability, or even toxic emotions as you could harm your soul.

43: Sabnock

MARQUIS

Color: Violet
Incense: Jasmine
Metal: Silver
Planet: Moon
Element: Fire

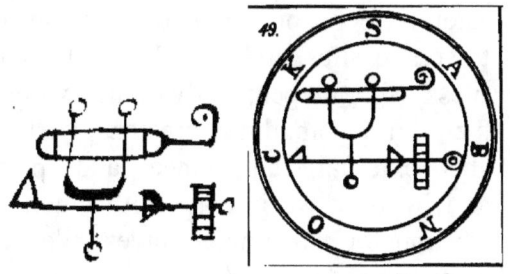

*The 43ᵈ spirit in order as Solomon commanded them into the Brazen vessel is called **Sabnach (Sabnock).** He is a mighty great marquis, and strong appearing in the form of an armed soldier with a lion's head, riding on a pale colored horse. His office is to build high towers, castles, and cities, and to furnish them with armor. And to afflict men several days with wounds and rotten sores full of worms. He gives good familiars at the command of the exorcist. He commands 50 legions of spirits.*

The Alchemical Breakdown:

Within Sabock's seal, we find the symbols for silver, day and night, fire (or a gentle fire), gold, purification (and red arsenic), putrefaction (could be iron or incineration), arsenic sulfide or a gold color or pigment. At first glance it looks like a recipe for adding gold leaf or gold plating to another metal to make it appear as gold using a red colored arsenic. After all, it was the early alchemists who did eventually figure out how to gold-plate other substances, as with gilding, in the late medieval period and early renaissance. A lot of our metallurgy and chemistry knowledge today was spurred by alchemists of this time period.

The spiritual process described could be that we transform ourselves a little at a time, and by transforming the outer layer, ultimately, we become transformed inwardly. You can build "towers, castles, and cities" as well as armor, but it is all useless without people dwelling within them to transform them into something greater. By focusing on changing the external appearance and presence of ourselves, and by how we interact with others and carry ourselves, we transform our inner selves. We become the behaviors we practice.

The lion, mentioned in the description, represents the individual ascension of the alchemist. To afflict men in several days with wounds and rotting sores full of worms sounds to me, again, like the kinds of injuries you might receive working with toxic substances like arsenic. This might include skin lesions and bumps, hard patches of skin on the palms and soles of feet, and darkening of the skin in patches. Prolonged exposure also could result in digestive issues. It could also suggest that this process could cause wounds that would get infected. That doesn't sound pleasant at all.

Spiritually, a lot of shadow work and working on the self in general, can open old wounds or traumas and cause them to fester. So, be sure to take care of any non-physical wounds that surface during spiritual alchemy, too. Processes of transformation, spiritually speaking, are never without risks including emotional pain, fear, upheaval, and even trauma.

44: Shax

MARQUIS

Color: Violet
Incense: Jasmine
Metal: Silver
Planet: Moon
Element: Air

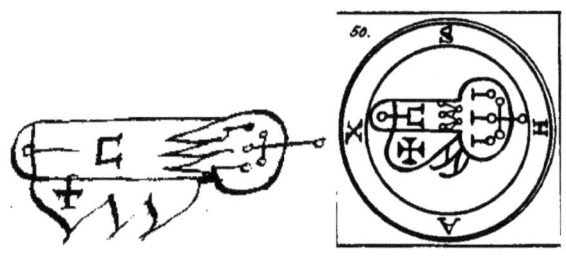

The 44th spirit is named **Shax.** *He is a great marquis and appears in the form of a stock dove, speaking with a hoarse and subtle voice. His office is to take away the sight, hearing, and understanding of any man or woman at the command of the exorcist, and to steal money out of king's houses. And carry it again in 1200 years, if commanded. He will fetch horses or anything at the request of the exorcist, but he must be commanded into a triangle first, or else he will deceive him, and tell you many lies. He can discover all things that are hidden and not kept by wicked spirits. He gives good familiars sometimes, and he governs 30 legions of spirits.*

The Alchemical Breakdown:

In this seal we see symbols for silver (or metallic mercury which was silver in color), vinegar, sulfur, day, distillation apparatus, and digestion. There is also a symbol here that could represent gold, or potentially alumen saccharinum, which is a substance used in tanning leather. While I doubt this is a recipe for tanning leather, I suspect this could have been a recipe for some type of transformative elixir. Oftentimes, just looking at the ingredients and what they symbolize can help us in instances where the recipe isn't straight forward or clearly apparent. Some of these sigils are very clear in their meaning. Others are more subtle, such as the components within Shax's seal.

Vinegar is an acid, and gently dissolves barriers. Silver is the metal that indicates reflection, divination, and insight into emotions. Metallic Mercury is the bridge between matter and spirit. Gold, of course, represents ascension of the highest and the transformation being complete. Even though Shax has a lot of watery correspondences – there's also an airy quality. This could suggest that this is a recipe for dealing with the emotions of reflection through philosophy and thinking. Shax can help us reflect through observation rather than through feeling. This is further supported by the fact that he must be summoned into the triangle of art. The triangle contains a black mirror within it, so that one can look at the self outwardly, and gradually see what hides beneath.

The spirit first appears as a dove – a symbol of the soul and its journey from ignorance to enlightenment. When one begins their journey, they may be blind and deaf and lack any understanding. But as the alchemist reflects on the self, and observes the self, they gain understanding. They can see more clearly. They can hear what others are communicating. It is, essentially, a recipe for self-knowledge, which leads to emotional control and emotional intelligence.

When it comes to the triangle -- if you don't look within, you could by lying to yourself. *He will fetch horses or anything at the request of the exorcist, but he must be commanded into the triangle* – he can do anything he puts his mind to if he knows himself. *He can discover all things that are hidden* – refers to wisdom. *Wicked spirits* could be a code term for self-sabotage, and the designation *wicked spirits* did not mean malevolent entities; they symbolized the darker aspects of existence and the self—the chaotic, unpredictable forces that resisted transformation. Since the Ars Goetia is a book of wicked spirits, it's basically a book of darker alchemical recipes for deep shadow work.

Together with mercury (symbolizing femininity, moisture, and cold) and salt, sulfur forms the *Three Primes*—fundamental components in alchemical philosophy. Though, sadly, salt is not found symbolically in the seal. Instead, we find the combination of the masculine sulfur with the feminine liquid mercury, suggesting a balance between the mental and the emotional.

45: Vine

KING

Color: Yellow
Incense: Frankincense
Metal: Gold
Planet: Sun
Element: Water

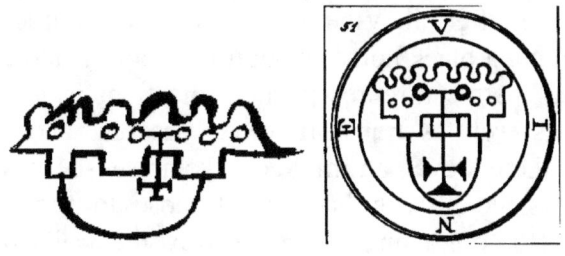

The 45 spirit is called **Vine**. He is a great king and earl, and appears in the form of a lion riding on a black horse with a viper in his hand. His office is to discover things hidden, witches, and things present past and to come. He, at the command of the exorcist, will build towers, throw down great stone walls, make waters rough with storms and, he governs 35 legions of spirits.

The Alchemical Breakdown:

Vine is another one of those seals that eluded me for some time. It includes the alchemical symbols of white arsenic (arsenic album), vinegar, water, aqua fortis (strong water or nitric acid), purification, and either calcination or filtration. Again, some symbols have dual meanings depending on the symbol set you're using. This could be a recipe for an aqua fortis elixir, to spiritually break down inner walls that the alchemist has built around their traumas. Because there is a lot of water symbolism in the seal, correspondences, and descriptions, this suggests that this particular part of shadow work deals with breaking down the emotional walls we've built to protect ourselves in order to hide from our fears and traumas.

With trace amounts of arsenic, plenty of water, and nitric acid – an elixir made from these ingredients would symbolically help one face these fears and traumas. In the description, after all, Vine comes as a lion (journey of the soul), riding a black horse (inhabiting a body), and carrying a viper. Vipers can represent the protections we carry (our walls), as well as transformation, wisdom, and healing. Perhaps there's even an implied psychic self-defense angle to Vine since he can both build those towers we hide ourselves or our pain in, and destroy the walls of those same towers. He can also make *waters* (emotions) *rough with storms* (emotional turbulence).

Sometimes towers are useful, like when we're under attack from external forces. Sometimes, however, they harbor the beasts within us that we need to deal with, confront, and conquer.

46: Bifrons

EARL

Color: Red
Incense: Dragon's Blood
Metal: Copper or Silver
Planet: Mars
Element: Earth

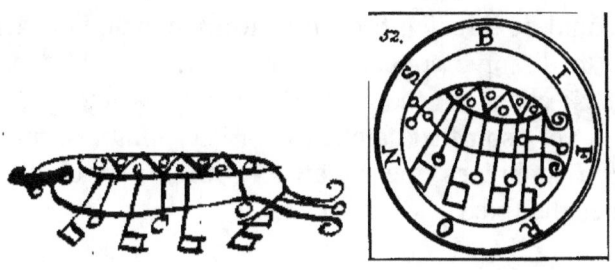

*The 46th spirit is called **Bifrons**. He is an earl and appears in the form of a monster at first, but after a while at the command of the exorcist he puts on the shape of a man. His office is to make one knowing in astrology and geometry, and other arts and sciences. And he teaches the virtues of all herbs, precious stones and woods. He changes the dead bodies and puts them into one another's places, and lights candles seemingly upon the graves of the dead. He has under his command 6 Legions of spirits.*

The Alchemical Breakdown:

The first thing you may notice is that the seal itself looks like a bug. Perhaps a grasshopper or beetle of some sort. Bugs generally represent metamorphosis and change. In the seal itself we have a lot of information. The alchemical symbols for layer-upon-layer appears, as well as the symbol of cuprum citrinum (gold color alloys of copper) or possibly sublimate of verdigris (copper acetate). The alchemical symbols of sulfur or vitriol, and one ounce, as well as silver and distillation also occur. The symbols for fixed and not fixed also make up the bug body. The overall shape of our little bug looks to potentially be a symbol for salt, and there's also the symbol for aqua fortis (nitric acid). It's even possible that one of the symbols could be for flowers. As you can see, there's a great deal going on here.

This could be a recipe for a transformative aqua fortis or a recipe to dissolve copper and/or silver. A fixed substance becomes changed (non-fixed), which is the repetitive process of spiritual alchemy. Everything is in flux. Fixation stabilizes the volatile, while the volatilization liberates the fixed.

But deeper than that – the corrosive nature of aqua fortis and the process of dissolving metals is a spiritual metaphor for the process of facing our inner impurities, dissolving ego-driven barriers, and emerging transformed.

Bifrons is another one of the Ars Goetia's "death Daemonic" or divine intelligences that rule over death. As mentioned in the description, he *changes the dead bodies* and lights candles on the graves of the dead. Of course, this could be rather symbolic of that change or transformation. In the description we also have the mention of the monster that turns into a man. The "monster" in alchemy transcends mere physical appearance; it embodies hidden truths, cosmic forces, and the alchemist's inner journey while also suggesting metamorphosis, just like bugs and beetles.

Transformation and metamorphosis can also describe the process of death and decay. It all changes form. The body returns back to earth, the soul is transformed and liberated. **Death spirits** are **change spirits**.

This makes me think of the natural cyclic nature of all things. All living animals are born, we live, we reproduce, we die. Seeds germinate, grow, form new seeds, and the parent plants eventually die. All life follows this cycle of birth, life, and death and it begins anew. The process or recipe the seal of Bifrons reveals is clearly one that involves knowledge of herbs, stones/minerals, and wood (from which certain alchemical substances are made).

47: Uvall

DUKE

Color: Green
Incense: Sandalwood
Metal: Copper
Planet: Venus
Element: Water
(Also Vual)

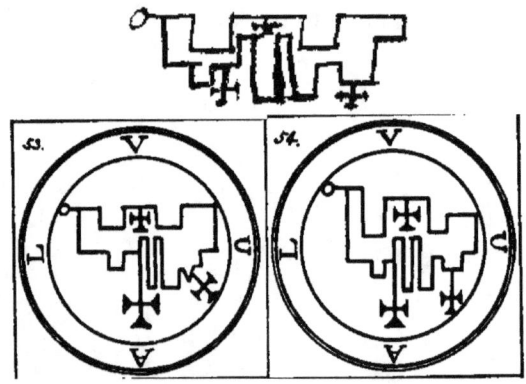

*The 47th spirit is called **Vual (or Uvall)**. He is a great and mighty strong duke. He appears in the form of a mighty dromedary (camel) at first, but after a while he puts on human shape, and speaks in the Egyptian tongue, but not perfectly. His office is to procure the love of women, and to tell things past, present and to come, and to procure friendship between friends and foes. He was of the order of potentates and he governs 37 legions of spirits.*

The Alchemical Breakdown:

Included in the alchemical symbols found in this seal are calcination, vinegar or acid, day, Venus, salt, potash, Aqua Regis, and potentially a symbol for sulfur. The problem with seals that contain multiple geometric symbols that contain squares or rectangles is that whoever put together the seals, ran the symbols together to create the emblem which can make decoding the seal a bit more challenging.

This appears to be a recipe for a "Salt of Venus" or an "Elixir of Venus" perhaps symbolic of healing the heart. To make the potash, one would calcinate wood, then boil the ashes in a copper pot. Potash was used in a multitude of ways from making soap, fertilizer, and glass to bleaching textiles, dying fabrics, and as a leavening agent in baking. So, it would stand to reason that the potash was the salt of the calcination of wood, and added to vinegar distilled from wine, might be turned into an elixir or salt of Venus that was taken internally as a symbolic heart healing.

The use of the dromedary (camel) symbolism in the description suggests the physical world, earth, fertility, and perhaps even a connection between the mind and spirit to the physical body. It also suggests endurance. This spirit is all about friendship, reconciliation and love – all emotional and water based. The Venusian and watery symbolism could also extend to seeing the past, present, and future by way of intuition of the heart. Knowing by trusting what your heart tells you – especially when it comes to relationships between the alchemist and the people around them.

48: Haagenti

PRESIDENT

Color: Orange
Incense: Storax
Metal: Mercury
Planet: Mercury
Element: Earth (Water)

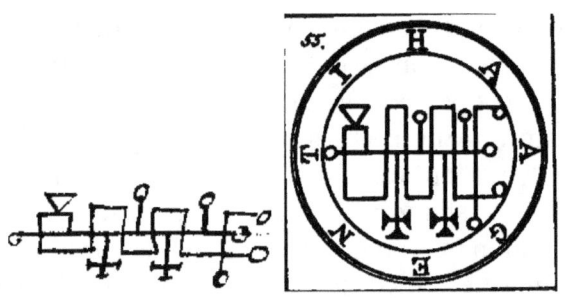

The 48th spirit is called **Haagenti.** *He is a great president appearing in the form of a mighty bull with griffin's wings at first. But afterwards, at the command of the Exorcist, he puts on human shape and his office is to make men wise and to instruct them in diverse things and to transmute all metals into gold, and change wine into water, and water into wine. He commands 33 legions of spirits.*

The Alchemical Breakdown:

Within Haagenti's seal, we find the symbols for night and day, arsenic, water, fire, earth (antimony) and salt. In the description, the spirit is a mighty bull (representing earth) with griffin's wing's – the griffin being associated with the process of sublimation. Sublimation happens when a substance transitions directly from a solid to a gaseous state without passing through the liquid phase. Symbolically, it represents the purification and elevation of the soul or the refinement of materials. This aligns with the Mercurial nature of Haagenti based on his correspondences.

If we consider the griffin's association with sublimation and the symbols contained within Haagenti's seal, it's possible to interpret them within the context of the sublimation process.

Night and Day could represent the initial dissolution phase (night) and the subsequent coagulation or solidification phase (day) of the alchemical process. Arsenic might symbolize the material or substance to be subjected to the sublimation process. (Perhaps fears, toxic traits, or traumas.) Water, Fire, Earth (or Antimony), and Salt: These elements could represent the various stages or aspects of the sublimation process. Water and fire could symbolize the heating and vaporization stages, while earth (or antimony) and salt could symbolize the solidification and collection stages. Thus, the transformation or purification of any internal toxic habits or traits the alchemist wishes to transform.

Since Haagenti is a spirit of transformation – turning metals to gold and water to wine (and vice versa), we could also simply interpret the spirit and his seal as being representative of alchemical transformation overall, or the manipulation of substances (shadow self).

49: Crocell

DUKE

Color: Green
Incense: Sandalwood
Metal: Copper
Planet: Venus
Element: Water

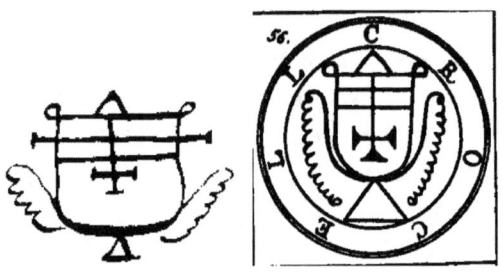

*The 49th spirit is named **Procel (or Crocell)**. He appears in the form of an angel, he is a great and strong duke, speaking something mystically of hidden things. He teaches the art of geometry and liberal sciences. At the command of the Exorcist, he will make great noises, like the running of great waters, although there be none. He warms waters and distempers baths and he was of the order of potentates (as he declared to Solomon) before his fall. He governs 48 legions of spirits.*

The Alchemical Breakdown:

Crocell's seal contains the alchemical symbols for purification, fire, arsenic, vinegar, verdigris (copper acetate), strong fire, and sulfur. I could not find any alchemical recipes that contained these particular ingredients, but it has become clear to me, as I am writing this book, that even the ingredients are symbolic of spiritual alchemical processes even if there are no laboratory alchemical recipe equivalents that I can find for every seal.

Speculatively speaking – this could be a recipe for the purification of copper (transformation and balance) in that these symbols could be interpreted metaphorically, representing inner processes of transformation, purification, and enlightenment guided by the spirit Crocell.

To break it down more completely, the purification symbol suggests a process of refining or purifying a substance, which aligns with Crocell's association with teaching and knowledge. The presence of fire above and below indicates the transformative nature of the work, both on a spiritual and physical level. Arsenic, vinegar, verdigris, and sulfur could represent materials or substances involved in the alchemical operations guided by Crocell, again, possibly related to the transformation or purification of copper or other metals. The strong fire symbol suggests the use of intense heat in the alchemical process. Perhaps the intensity of passion or emotion? While warming water and distempering baths could represent further spiritual purification and renewal.

Angels in alchemy can represent multiple things, including divine guidance, suggesting that Crocell's guidance is divine guidance over these transformations of emotion. Spiritually speaking, this is a recipe for tempering strong or volatile emotions for renewal and bringing balance back to one's emotional state.

50: Furcas

KNIGHT

Color: Black
Incense: Myrrh
Metal: Lead
Planet: Saturn
Element: Air
(Also Furcus)

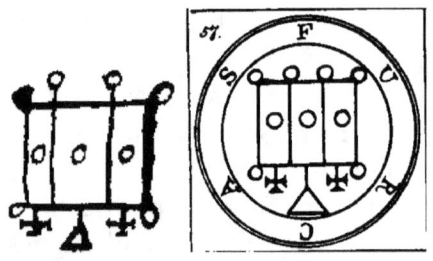

The 50th spirit in order is called **Furcas.** *He is a knight and appears in the form and similitude of a cruel old man with a long beard and a gray head, sitting on a pale-colored horse, with a sharp weapon in his hand. His office is to teach the arts of philosophy, astronomy, rhetoric, logic, chiromancy, and pyromancy in all their parts perfectly. He has under his power 20 legions of spirits.*

The Alchemical Breakdown:

The alchemical symbols in this seal include arsenic (of course), gold, fire, vinegar, night, and lead. While again I couldn't find any particular recipes that used these ingredients, my best guess is this is a recipe to turn lead to gold. Though it could just as easily be a recipe for the philosopher's stone, or could be how to extract mercury (air) from its natural ore using vinegar in a lead mortar. Both would make sense to some degree because the description of the spirit suggests extracting knowledge from teachers or books.

In a sense, Furcas could also help open the mind and make one curious. Saturn, the planet of hard work, also falls in line with the work that must be done to secure an education.

Also in the description, there is mention of Furcas riding upon a pale horse, and he himself is sporting a gray beard. Horses in alchemy are symbolic of the four elements and may suggest foundation and balance. The mention of paleness and gray leads me to think of the color white. Associated with the second stage of the alchemical work, albedo or whitening as this stage is referred to, is where the alchemist washes and cleanses the matter, separates the pure from the impure, and the matter emerges as something new. This could be a metaphor for critical thinking, which is always useful when you're learning new things.

51: Balam

KING

Color: Yellow
Incense: Frankincense
Metal: Gold
Planet: Sun
Element: Earth

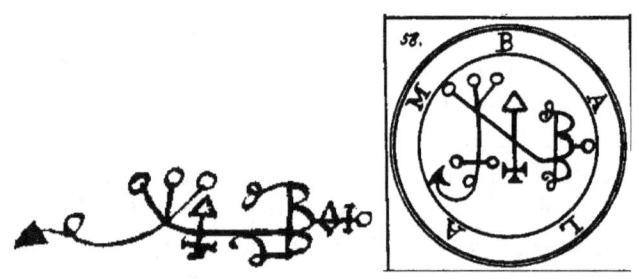

The 51st spirit is **Balam.** He is a terrible, great, and powerful king, appearing with 3 heads. The first is like a bull's, the second like a man's, and the third like a ram's head. He has a serpent's tail, and eyes flaming. He rides upon a furious bear, carrying a hawk on his fist. He speaks with a hoarse voice, giving true answers of things past present and to come. He makes men to go invisible and witty. He governs 40 legions of spirits.

The Alchemical Breakdown:

This seal includes the alchemical symbols for sulfur, one ounce, steel or iron, distillation, ash, and potentially slow mild heat via horse dung, and the symbol for the work complete – to gold.

In this instance, iron could symbolize the base material undergoing transformation, whereas sulfur represents the soul. The mention of truth in the description of the spirit likely suggests being true to oneself. While I couldn't find any historical recipes including all of these things, I can conclude that Balam is a spirit that gives one insight into the truth of the self. Whether it's finding the authentic self, or the alchemist is analyzing himself and not lying to himself. Divination can give one insight.

This spirit appears with three heads. The first is that of a bull, representing earth and the bridge between mind, body, and spirit and the first part of the alchemical process where the matter is put to the fire for purification. The second head is a man's representing the self. The third is a ram – symbolizing the elements and a balanced foundation. He has a serpent's tail – representing wisdom and transformation, and flaming eyes – to see truth, no matter how painful. He rides upon a furious bear and carries a hawk. The bear symbolizing transformation, and the hawk symbolizing intuition and spiritual awareness.

The description and the seal together show a spirit that represents the initial alchemical process and embodies the phrase – man know thyself, and thou shalt know the gods. This is a spirit whose purpose it is to help the alchemist shine the scathing fire of reflection inwardly. It may even represent our inner critic and how, if used properly, the inner critic can facilitate self-transformation. The more one knows themselves, the easier it is to predict outcomes from actions, to see the truth of what has passed, and understand the present.

52: Alloces

DUKE

Color: Green
Incense: Sandalwood
Metal: Copper
Planet: Venus
Element: Fire

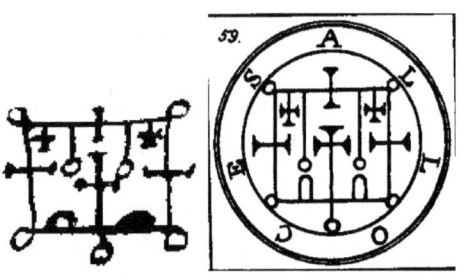

*The 52^d spirit is called **Alloces**. He is a great and mighty strong duke, appearing in the form of a soldier riding on a great horse; his face is like a lion's, very red, having eyes flaming. His speech is hoarse and very big. His office is to teach the art of astronomy, and all the liberal sciences. He brings good familiars and rules 36 legions of spirits.*

The Alchemical Breakdown:

Alloces' seal seems to be a statement more than a recipe. The included alchemical symbols in the emblem include acid, arsenic, spirit, calcination, day, copper, and the aurum potable.

The aurum potable, as mentioned many times within this book, was a drinkable gold that allegedly strengthened the body and spirit. The gold was dissolved in the aqua regis (hydrochloric and nitric acids), then added to rainwater. It's also plausible that this dissolved gold could be added, in trace amounts, to other distilled spirits to create more medicinal preparations. The preparation of elixirs in this manner is akin to modern homeopathy, where substances that might normally be dangerous to ingest, like arsenic, were broken down (usually via calcination) and added, in small amounts, to other substances so that only trace amounts (if any) of the original compound remained, thus rendering its ingestion relatively harmless to the human body. That said, it was believed these elixirs were very potent and powerful despite what little was left of the original compound.

In the description, Alloces is said to appear as a soldier riding on a great horse. The soldier's face appears as a lion's with the mention of it being very red, and with eyes flaming. His office is to teach astronomy and all the liberal sciences and to bring good familiars to the alchemist. Horses, again, symbolize the four elements. The lion represents ascension or enlightenment. Red is the beginning of the final stages of the alchemical work and is the completion and perfection of matter and the union of opposites.

The statement I mentioned previously might go something like – by embarking on the alchemical process, creating the drinkable gold, and strengthening the body and spirit, one becomes more confident and courageous in oneself and one's knowledge, and ascends – bringing opportunity and assistance as needed. Confident alchemists, after all, may have all kinds of people with information and assistance (familiars) flocking to them. Not only helping them gain more knowledge, but also giving them great insight, helping them to ascend even further. Broken down, that statement might be – do the self-work of breaking things down and bringing it all back together in a more balanced way where it's no longer harmful, then drink in the knowledge and company of others, and gain great wisdom and enlightenment.

53: Caim

PRESIDENT

Color: Orange
Incense: Storax
Metal: Mercury
Planet: Mercury
Element: Fire
(Also Camio)

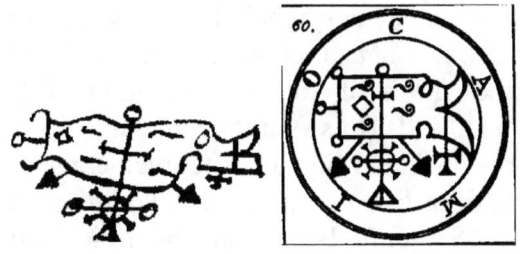

The 53^d spirit is called **Caim.** *He is a great president and appears in the form of a bird called a thrush at first. But after a while he puts on the shape of a man carrying in his hand a sharp sword. He seems to answer in burning ashes. He is a good disputer. His office is to give men the understanding of all birds, lowing of bulls, barking of dogs, and other creatures. And also, the noise of waters, and gives very true answers of things to come. He was of the order of angels, and now rules 30 legions of infernal spirits.*

The Alchemical Breakdown:

I can't help but feel that Caim, in some way, is a spirit that says, in his own way, shut up and actively listen and you will learn something. Especially nature. Rural people knew the rhythms of the land. They knew when the seasons would change by watching the animals and the weather. They knew when a cold front would come in, or when it might be unseasonably warm. They knew what was to come just by being in nature, watching, and listening to its rhythms.

In this seal we have the symbols for marcasite or metallum, silver, day, fire, soot/ash, copper, acid, gold, antimony (or gold colored alloys of copper) and ammoniac which is ammonium chloride (this symbol could also represent salt). Again, I was unable to find an exact recipe, but I did find a translation from *Farmaceutica Antimoniale Trionfo del Mercurio*, 1683, third book done by Iulia Millesima on labyrinthdesigners.org[1] that utilizes many of these substances depicted in the seal in the process for the sublimation of mercury. I suspect the symbols for silver within the seal are meant to suggest liquid mercury. This process does involve fire, salt, vinegar(acid), and vitriol (copper sulfate) to sublimate the mercury.

Caim appears as a bird – a messenger of the gods – who then transforms into the shape of man carrying a sword (air and wisdom). He answers in burning ashes – calcining matter to ash as the first step in many alchemical processes to separate the conscious mind from the unconscious mind. And yet sublimation also includes the process of high

---

[1] **Lancillotti, Operations on Mercury. Part 3 (labyrinthdesigners.org)** https://www.labyrinthdesigners.org/alchemy-ancient-chemistry/lancillotti-operations-on-mercury-part-3/

temperatures but refers to substances that don't melt to liquid as with calcination, and instead go directly from solid to gas. If you remove this liquid stage (which occurs in calcination but not in sublimation), one is technically removing emotion from the equation and is instead focusing on pure logical thought, and communication. This would, indeed, make one good at debating and give one a deeper understanding of nature. This observational stance would also bring truth and knowing without injecting feelings into the observation.

Caim is then, in essence, the separation of the emotional from the logical. Setting aside the ego and favoring actual observation and results over presumption and desire. Favoring science and experimentation over mere guessing or philosophizing.

54: Murmur

DUKE

Color: Green
Incense: Sandalwood
Metal: Copper
Planet: Venus
Element: Water (Fire)

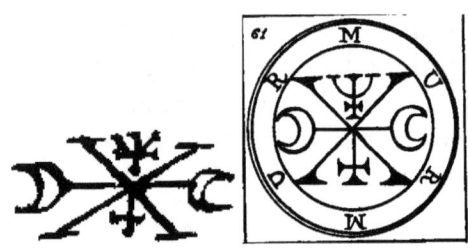

The 54th spirit is in order called **Murmur.** *He is a great duke and an earl and appears on the form of a soldier riding on a griffin with a duke's crown on his head. There go before him two of his ministers, with great trumpets sounding. His office is to teach philosophy perfectly, and to constrain souls deceased to come before the exorcist to answer those things yet he shall ask them, if he desires; he was partly of the order of Thrones and partly of angels, and rules now 30 legions of spirits.*

The Alchemical Breakdown:

Within this seal are symbols for copper, ash (likely from crushing), crucible, vinegar, metallic mercury, summer, and the moon-silver. To me, this suggests a recipe for extracting something, from beyond the realm of the living perhaps? One of the most common recipes for metallic mercury is how to extract it from cinnabar. The alchemists would grind cinnabar with vinegar in a copper mortar and pestle and as they did this, it would produce a blackish powder with the mercury floating on top.

I have erroneously tried to break down this seal in the past as a process of dissolution. But in the first seal, the top glyph looks more like a process of putrefaction. And in the newer seal, a process of extraction. If the older seal on the left is correct and that is, in fact, putrefaction of the metallic mercury in acid – it could suggest the breakdown and dissolution of impurities and the release of hidden energies/entities. So, even if I wasn't quite spot on in my previous suggestions of the seal's alchemy – I still think it stands to reason that Murmur is involved in breaking down, dissolving, and extracting. Whether it applies to the veil between worlds, or the barriers within us holding us back from reaching our full potential. As a Death Daemonic, Murmur is said to bring the dead back through to speak with the living. He also teaches philosophy.

In the description, Murmur appears as a crowned soldier riding a Griffin – a symbol of sublimation and the union of fire and air (hot fiery Venus and airy Mercury). On that same token, there is a watery element to Murmur, too in the symbolism of Silver and the moon in the seal. This suggests he connects with the alchemist's intuition as well – which is something necessary to communicate with the spirits of the dead.

For comparison, here was my initial translation of the seal from *Keys of Ocat*, before I had found the right symbol sets: *The symbol for the alchemical process of dissolution typically consists of a downward-pointing triangle or an upside down V with another leg down the middle, which represents water or the solvent, descending into a vessel or circle that contains the substance to be dissolved. In the case of Murmur's sigil, this is mirrored above and below. This symbol is used to represent the breaking down or dissolution of the ego, or the transformation of base matter into something new and pure. In the case of Murmur, it also suggests the dissolution of the veil between the world of the living and the dead, suggesting that Murmur can be rather useful during necromantic work, which makes sense since he is one of several Death Daemonic within the hierarchy of Goetic spirits. You will also notice the inclusion of the symbol for the moon mirrored on the right and left. The moon actually corresponds with water and silver, and in this case suggests that Murmur has an intuitive aspect, since the moon rules over intuition and emotion and even psychic powers such as mediumship and divination.*

Both interpretations come to similar conclusions.

55: Orobas

PRINCE

Color: Blue
Incense: Cedar
Metal: Tin
Planet: Jupiter
Element: Water

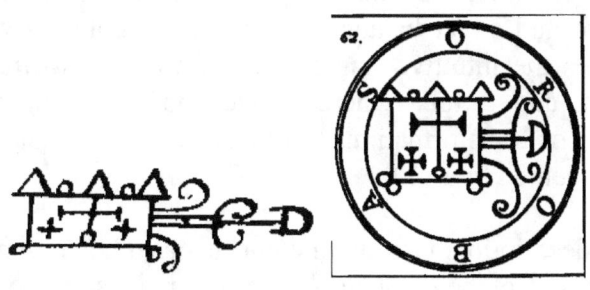

*The 55th spirit is called **Orobas**. He is a mighty great prince, appearing at first like a horse, but afterwards at the command of the exorcist he puts on the image of a man. His office is to discover all things past, present and to come, and to give dignities and prelacies and the favor of friends and foes. He gives true answers of divinity and of the creation of the world. He is faithful to the exorcist and will not suffer him to be tempted by any spirit. He governs 20 legions of spirits.*

The Alchemical Breakdown:

In Orobas' seal are the symbols for fire, gold, acid, the aurum potable, orpiment (which could also be a symbol for salt or horse dung – to heat a mixture) vitriol, Jupiter, lamina (thin slices or plates), digestion, and possibly silver and the moon. While I couldn't find any actual laboratory recipes including all these elements, what these ingredients do suggest is, perhaps, an ascension to wisdom. So, it could be an elixir for astral travel or dreamwork, healing, or the transmutation of consciousness and ultimately the ascension of the spirit.

To break it down more completely, tin would represent the earthly realm. Vinegar, as a solvent, would bridge the material to the ethereal, Fire would transmute the mundane to the sublime. The aurum potable symbolizes distilled wisdom and silver balances out the fiery gold, as well as provides the intuitive "sight" needed to see into the past, present, and future. Whereas digestion is the alchemical process of transformation. In this scenario – the alchemist is represented by tin.

In the description, Orobas first appears as a horse – the four elements. He then transforms into a man suggesting the foundation for the transformation. You can't have transformation without the base matter.

56: Gremory

DUKE

Color: Green
Incense: Sandalwood
Metal: Copper
Planet: Venus
Element: Water

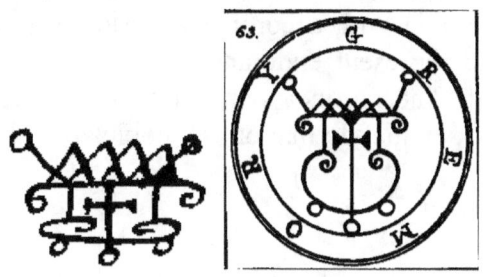

The 56th spirit is called **Gremory.** *He is a strong and powerful duke appearing in the form of a beautiful woman, with a duchess's coronet tied about her middle, riding on a great camel. His office is to tell of all things past, present, and to come, and of treasure hidden and whatever lies within. He procures the love of women, both young and old. He governs 26 legions of spirits.*

The Alchemical Breakdown:

What's interesting in the description is that Gremory begins as a woman and is suddenly referred to as 'he' and it brings up a very important point that these spirits and processes are only masculine or feminine in their alchemical reactions. Gremory is likely more in the feminine with softer Venusian and watery aspects. I feel like this seal actually details an elixir for love or attraction, and for divination.

In the seal itself you will see the symbols for water (could be camphor), red arsenic (which could also potentially be a liquid saline), copper, the aurum potable, the purification of gold, night, and possibly alumen.

The power of Venus attracts, whether love or wealth, and the watery aspects of Gremory promote the sight of a seer. In the description, we see that Gremory appears as a beautiful woman with a coronet and riding a camel. The camel could represent endurance and a connection to the spirit world. The coronet symbolizes nobility. Perhaps a statement to say that divination is a noble art?

57: Ose

PRESIDENT

Color: Orange
Incense: Storax
Metal: Mercury
Planet: Mercury
Element: Air

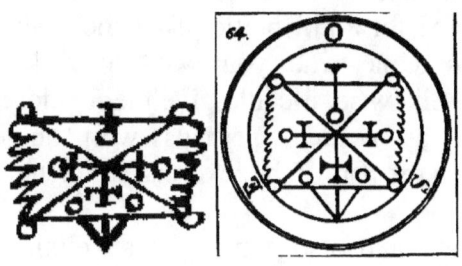

*The 57th spirit is called **Ose**. He is a great president and appears like a leopard at first. But after a little time, he puts on the shape of a man. His office is to make one cunning in the liberal sciences and to give true answers of divine and secret things. And to change a man into any shape that the exorcist desires so that he is so changed that he will not think he is any other thing; but that he is that creature or thing he is changed into. He governs 30 legions of spirits.*

The Alchemical Breakdown:

In this seal we have the symbols for gold, copper + iron (which could also be mercury or marcasite), the aurum potable, the aqua vitae, a strong fire, the symbol for an hour, mercury, and a tigillum or crucible. There is possibly the symbol for arsenic (or borax) in the seal, too. These ingredients suggest an elixir meant to heighten intuition or assist in a deeper connection to all that is. Perhaps trace amounts of the prepared toxic elements, with a drop of the aurum potable mixed into the aqua vitae (water of life) comprise this elixir.

In the description, you'll notice there is the suggestion that this recipe can be used to influence others. I suppose any excess consumption of alcohol might make one think one has transformed into something other than oneself. Perhaps this is a recipe for a gift bottle of alcohol, which could be given to someone who you want to make an ass of themselves. Likewise, it could give them a dose of courage or strength as needed, perhaps with an element of suggestion on the part of the 'exorcist' or alchemist.

That said, it could also simply be an elixir used before divination or meditation to help one connect with the higher self or powers that be. Perhaps it is all of these things.

Ose appears as a leopard at first and leopards symbolize regeneration, transformation, and the ability to manifest one's desires. Therefore, we could also postulate that the elixir could have healing benefits, too, hence aqua vitae.

58: Amy

PRESIDENT

Color: Orange
Incense: Storax
Metal: Mercury
Planet: Mercury
Element: Fire

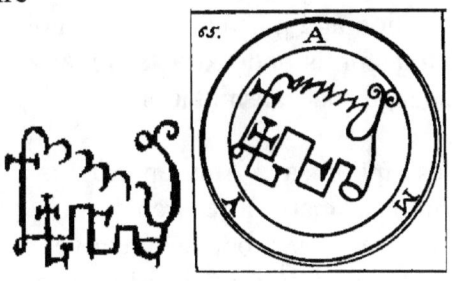

*The 58th spirit is called **Amy**. He is a great president and appears at first in the form of a flaming fire, but after a while he puts on the shape of a man. His office is to make one wondrously knowing in astrology and all the liberal sciences. He gives good familiars and can disclose treasures which are kept by spirits. He governs 36 legions of spirits.*

The Alchemical Breakdown:

Amy, the seal, looks like a cat or a lion. Cats represent hidden knowledge, and this is clearly mentioned in the description of Amy, so one has to wonder if the shape of the seal is a happy accident, or purposeful. Within the seal are included the symbols for metallic mercury, silver, quicksilver (or it could be a symbol for tin), vinegar, dissolution, fire, distillation, and sublimation (which could also be the symbol for spirit or alcohol).

This could very well be a recipe to ignite one's inner passions or creative energy. To increase motivation as it were.

Silver represents the reflective lunar energy required to go within to find this fire. Mercury is the volatile essence representing the fluidity of transformation. Vinegar is the acid for dissolution and purification. Alcohol, or the spirit, is fiery and transforms and extracts. Finally, the fire is a catalyst for change and transmutation.

The seal's description says Amy appears as a flaming fire then turns into a man. Fire transforms, purifies, and enlightens. It could symbolize creative inspiration, a spiritual awakening, or an inner passion. I feel I may be on the right track here for suggesting this could be an elixir used as a catalyst to change and to help people find their passions, creative fire, and just that inner fire that motivates.

59: Orias

MARQUIS

Color: Violet
Incense: Jasmine
Metal: Silver
Planet: Moon
Element: Air

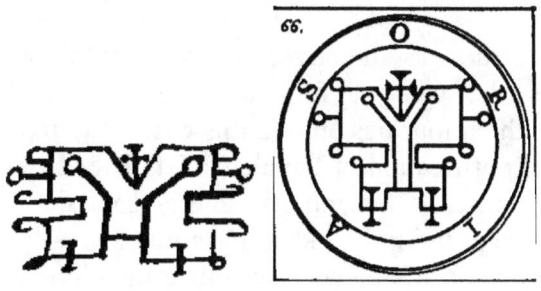

*The 59th spirit is named **Orias**. He is a great marquis and appears in the form of a lion, riding on a mighty horse, with a serpents tail, holding in his right hand 2 great serpents hissing. His office is to teach the virtues of the stars and to know the mansions of the planets, and how to understand their virtues. Also, he transforms men and gives dignities and prelacies, and confirmations, and the favor of friends and foes. He governs 30 legions of spirits.*

The Alchemical Breakdown:

Orias, for as long as I've known him, has always been a spirit of mental transformation. He changes one's perspective and helps them develop the right mindset for the changes one wishes to make. Let's see if the seal agrees. In this seal we have a great number of symbols. The symbols for projection, filter, night, vitriol, copper sulphate (or possible salt peter), silver and the moon, acid/vinegar, and the spirit of alcohol (or possibly sublimation).

From this it appears this might be a recipe for an elixir that, through distillation and filtration, removes acidic emotions and thoughts, leading to a more open mind which promotes learning, emotional control, and patience – not to mention emotional healing on some level.

To break it down - the silver represents intuition, and the vitriol is the catalyst for the transformation. Vinegar dissolves the impurities and, in this case, may represent the emotional purification of the alchemist. The alcohol adds a spiritual essence. The copper sulfate or potassium nitrate is the alchemical union of metal and minerals. And finally – projection could be included to infuse the elixir with lunar transformative energy.

In the description of the spirit, Orias appears as a lion – individual ascension or enlightenment. Riding on a horse – the four elements. With a serpent's tail and carrying 2 great serpents in his right hand - wisdom. This could suggest that enlightenment comes through the work and practice of healing the emotional self, adjusting one's thoughts, and transforming the self through this process. So yes, it seems the seal and other symbolism in the spirit's description supports what I've always said about Orias.

60: Vapula

DUKE

Color: Green
Incense: Sandalwood
Metal: Copper
Planet: Venus
Element: Air

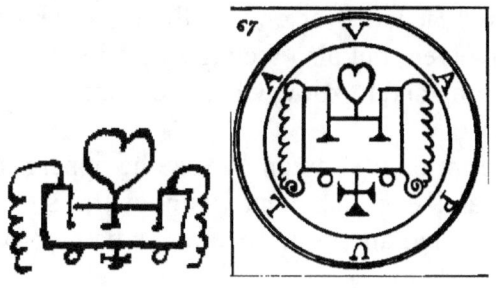

*The 60th spirit is called **Vapula**. He is a great mighty and strong duke, appearing in the form of a lion, with griffin's wings. His office is to make men knowing in all handicraft professions and also in philosophy and other sciences. He governs 36 legions of spirits.*

The Alchemical Breakdown:

Years ago, I had a friend who felt very connected with Vapula because she was a crafter. I have some ideas as to why crafters might feel a kinship with Vapula.

In the seal, we have the symbols for gold, gold-colored alloys of copper, strong fire, potash (from wood ash), and projection. To break this down – the gold represents the sun as well as enlightenment and the philosopher's stone. The gold-colored alloys of copper signify the blending of both earthly and celestial energy. Potash dissolves impurities and acts as a spiritual purification. Strong fire represents the transformation, or the alchemical forge where the transformation occurs. Finally, projection suggests infusing the elixir recipe this seal might divulge, with solar-transformative energies.

Some notes I made on Vapula after seeing the symbols: Apply heat/fire to the mind to teach the trades or sciences. To learn by doing and to refine skills over and over until expertise is reached. Not only is there an element of fiery passion involved, but also a clarity of mind to absorb what one is learning and to know what one wants to do.

In the description of Vapula, we see he appears as a lion – ascension and enlightenment, with griffin's wings – the union of fire and air (in motivation or passion for learning or doing).

This could, essentially be an elixir that attracts a passion for learning or creating, and helps broaden the mind to help one learn or create.

61: Zagan

KING

Color: Yellow
Incense: Frankincense
Metal: Gold
Planet: Sun
Element: Earth

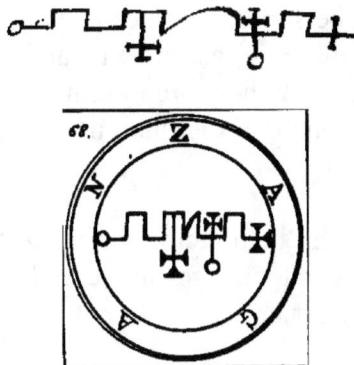

The 61st spirit is called **Zagan**. He is a great king and president, and appears at first in the form of a bull with griffin's wings, but afterwards he puts on human shape. He makes men witty. He can turn wine into water, and blood into wine, and also water into wine. He can turn all metals into coin of that dominion the metals are of and can make fools wise. He governs 33 legions of spirits.

The Alchemical Breakdown:

Zagan is the spirit that a lot of modern magicians work with if they need a life overhaul to turn a bad life situation into something more positive. Magicians are sometimes warned from this spirit just because the transformation reported by practitioners suggest the changes can often be profound and life altering, and if one isn't ready for them, one shouldn't be working with Zagan. Let's see if the seal backs this up.

Within the seal we see the symbols for acid/vinegar, Venus and copper, day, alcohol (or sublimation as the symbols look alike), the sun, gold, calcination, alumen, and distillation. I believe the Venusian elements are present in the seal to attract the transformation. Let's break things down. In this case, the vinegar might suggest emotional purification via dissolution. Venus and copper both attract and transform. The sun illuminates and enlightens. Gold is the ultimate goal – ascension and enlightenment. Calcination and alumen represent purification and crystallization. Finally, distillation is refinement and separation.

This could very well be a recipe for a transformative elixir meant to bring great change and enlightenment through solar and Venusian energies.

This is further solidified in the description where Zagan appears as a bull with griffin's wings. The bull – symbolic of earth and the first stage of the alchemical work (contrasted with gold – which is the final stage of enlightenment and perfection), and the griffin's wings which unite fire and air via sublimation.

All of this lends credence to the efficacy of Zagan, and this solar elixir of Zagan meant to bring about transformation and change.

62: Valac

PRESIDENT

Color: Orange
Incense: Storax
Metal: Mercury
Planet: Mercury
Element: Earth
(Also Volac)

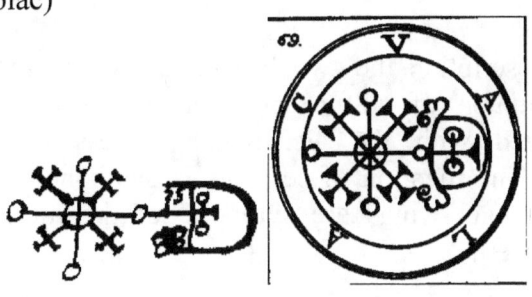

*The 62^d spirit is called **Valac**. He is a mighty great president and appears like a boy with angel's wings, riding on a 2 headed dragon. His office is to give true answers of hidden treasures, and to tell where serpents may be seen, which he will bring and deliver to the exorcist without any force or strength. He governs 30 legions of spirits.*

The Alchemical Breakdown:

Valac's seal contains the symbols for gold calcinated with mercury, mercury, iron sulphate, white clay, vinegar/acid, and salt (possibly urine). The iron is the earthy part, and clearly there is a lot of mercury here as it appears twice in two different symbols. This could, potentially be an elixir for unlocking astral gates, unveiling hidden desire, physical regeneration through easing the mind, or simply the transmutation of the soul. Or possibly, and it could be more simplistic – an elixir to bring balance to the mind, body, and soul of the magician in preparation for transmutation.

Breaking it down, the calcinated gold is the divine essence while mercury is the volatile spirit that bridges the material and the spiritual. Iron could be the hidden fire within, the catalyst for transformation. White clay has an earthy, grounding quality, while vinegar dissolves boundaries. The salt (perhaps within urine) could represent the essence of life.

In the description the two headed dragon represents the volatile union of sulfur and mercury, which must be harmonized with the alchemical process to maintain balance. The mention of serpents is symbolic of wisdom and the angel wings are symbolic of the transmutation process itself.

I am also reminded here that Mercury corresponds with Azoth – which comes from the Latin and Arabic meaning, *The Mercury*. Though initially it was coined as its own substance, a universal solvent, it was an esoteric formula pursued by alchemists and symbolized by the Caduceus.

63: Andras

MARQUIS

Color: Violet
Incense: Jasmine
Metal: Silver
Planet: Moon
Element: Air (Fire)

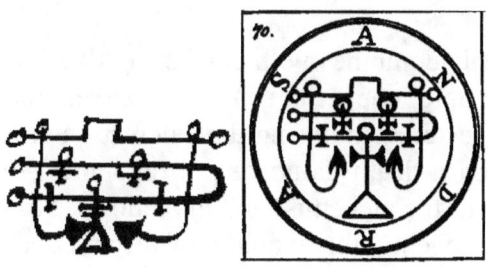

*The 63rd spirit is called **Andras**. He is a great marquis appearing in the form of an angel with a head like a black night raven, riding upon a black strong wolf, with a sharp bright sword flourishing in his hand. His office is to sow discords, if the exorcist hath not a care he will kill him and his fellows. He governs 30 legions of spirits.*

The Alchemical Breakdown:

How come I have a feeling this is another potentially toxic alchemical recipe judging by the description alone? Andras' seal contains the symbols for a copper or brass cremator, calcination, copper, gold-colored copper alloys, silver, the moon, alcohol, fire, and arsenic. This suggests some type of Lunar Elixir for aligning the soul with the divine and gaining divine insight. That said, it could also be a recipe to transmute base metals into radiant alloys and spiritually transmute man into a radiant divine being.

Now, looking at the description we have the angel, which symbolizes volatile matter. The Raven transforms matter through decomposition. The wolf is the animalistic part of man that must be tamed in order for transformation to occur. The sword is symbolic of purification and could be used to cut through the unknown leading to a deeper understanding of reality and truth.

When arsenic combines with copper or silver, it transforms the metals into copper arsenide or silver arsenide. The arsenic fumes created during the calcination process would have created a death cloud of poison fumes – that would definitely kill the alchemist and his fellows. So, in practical laboratory alchemy, this would sow discord and potentially lead to death if the recipe were followed – hence the warning of discord and death in the description.

On a spiritual alchemical level, it's almost as if this recipe facilitates the death or decomposition of the parts of the self that hinder the divine self. It would bring revelation and rebirth. My notes on this say: to burn away the parts no longer serving you, to transform one thing to another. To be reborn and to ascend. Refinement of the self, breaking down and perfecting the self – which can cause discord and chaos.

The meanings of the ingredients seem to agree with this as calcination breaks down impurities, copper suggests inner refinement, the gold-colored copper alloys symbolize spiritual illumination, and silver symbolizes reflection, intuition, and hidden knowledge.

64: Haures

DUKE

Color: Green
Incense: Sandalwood
Metal: Copper
Planet: Venus
Element: Fire
(Also Flauros)

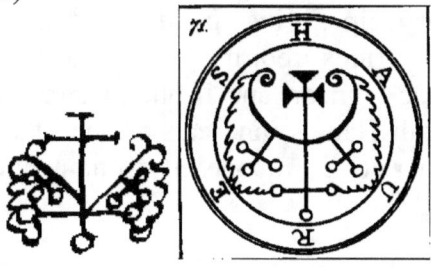

The 64th spirit is named **Flauros or Haures**. He is a great duke and appears at first like a mighty terrible and strong leopard but afterwards at the command of the Exorcist he puts on the shape of a man with fiery eyes and a terrible countenance. He gives true answers of all things past present and to come, but unless he be commanded into a triangle, he will lie in all those things and deceive or beguile the exorcist in other things or business. He will gladly talk of divinity, and of the creation of the world, and of his and all other spirit's fall. He destroys and burns those that are the exorcist's enemies if he requests it and will not suffer him to be tempted by any spirit or otherwise. He governs 36 legions of spirits.

The Alchemical Breakdown:

Haures' seal includes the symbols for copper, the aurum potable, vitriol, purification (in the 2nd seal), fire (in the first seal) or to flow, as well as the symbol for a strong fire. My initial notes on Haures say: purification by fire or fire baptism.

I was drawn to vitriol in this seal. There are three types: iron sulfate, sulfuric acid, and cobalt sulfate. The definition of vitriol is cruel and bitter criticism. This makes me think this particular recipe, brings painful truth and honesty that destroys and brings rebirth in its wake. The triangle contains a black mirror, and if one presumably looks into the mirror with Haures, one cannot deny the truth of the self. It's easier to lie to oneself without having to look oneself in the eye.

In the description we have the imagery of the leopard – the power of transformation and regeneration – and also a symbol of fire, who then becomes a man with fiery eyes and a terrible countenance. Perhaps suggesting viewing oneself with a discerning and critical eye and causing such revelation that one has no choice but to change and become reborn.

65: Andrealphus

MARQUIS

Color: Violet
Incense: Jasmine
Metal: Silver
Planet: Moon
Element: Air

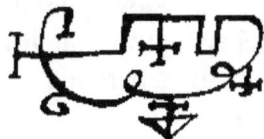 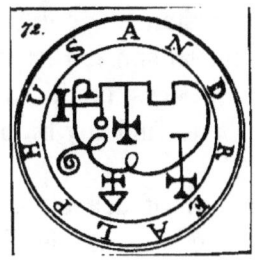

*The 65th spirit is called **Andrealphus**. He is a Mighty great marquis appearing at first in the form of a peacock, with great noises but afterward he puts on human shape. He can teach perfectly geometry, and all things belonging to measuring, also astronomy. He makes men very subtle and cunning therein. He can transform a man into the likeness of a bird and he governs 30 legions of spirits.*

The Alchemical Breakdown:

Andrealphus' seal contains the symbols for aqua fortis (strong water – nitric acid), vinegar, silver, ash (or firmus equinus, which is horse dung and was used in alchemy to slowly heat mixtures or was burned to ash and added to the recipe), and filtration. As I've said before, since we don't have the exact symbol set used for the alchemist(s) who created the Ars Goetia and the Lemegeton, we are stuck using whatever we can find in the same time period, and therefore, some of the symbols were challenging to discern. That said – we can make educated guesses as to what the author(s) were trying to say. In this instance, this recipe appears to suggest a slow and gradual transformation.

The aqua fortis symbolizes the power of dissolution and purification. The vinegar in this instance could be transformed through fermentation. Silver could represent (self) reflective qualities to develop intuition and uncover hidden knowledge. The ash, likely from burned horse dung in this instance, could represent a slow gradual transformation spurred by a gentle alchemical fire, and the filtration process could be indicative of separation and purification to find any hidden essences.

In the realm of academic study, this could suggest that studying and slow, methodic learning brings knowledge. In the spiritual realm, it suggests slow, methodic learning about the self, and separating and purifying the self, leads to a wiser, emotionally mature and intelligent person.

In the description, Andrealphus appears as a peacock – the ennoble aspect of matter. In alchemical terms, the process of transformation and elevation, whether of matter or the spirit, can be a form of ennoblement – or elevating something to a degree of respect or excellence. He can transform man into the likeness of a bird – the transformed alchemist.

66: Cimeies

MARQUIS

Color: Violet
Incense: Jasmine
Metal: Silver
Planet: Moon
Element: Earth
(Also Cimejes)

*The 66th spirit is called **Cimeies**. He is a mighty great marquis, strong and powerful. Appearing like a valiant soldier, riding on a goodly black horse, he rules over all spirits in the parts of Africa. His office is to teach perfectly grammar, rhetoric and logic and to discover treasures and things lost or hidden. He can make a man seem like a soldier of his own likeness. He governs 20 legions of chief spirits, but more inferior than himself.*

The Alchemical Breakdown:

The seal for Cimeies has within it the symbols for fire, night, vinegar/acid, filtration, a distillate – possibly aqua vitae (water of life), the symbol for to flow or drip, and the symbol for ½ ounce. There is a clear measurement here, so it's somehow important to the recipe.

In the description, Cimeies appears riding a black horse, symbolizing the elements and the first stage of the alchemical work. What is most interesting about the seal and the description is there is no mention of intuition, emotion, or anything that might suggest that watery moon energy – except for the fact that all the ingredients appear to be liquid in nature. Instead, we're left with earth as the element and my immediate thought here was that perhaps the recipe called for filtration through warm sand.

What I take away from this is that this could suggest that aqua vitae made with a touch of vinegar distilled from wine, just a half an ounce, can calm the mind enough to learn and expand the mind or to give one enough confidence (as a soldier) to complete a task.

If this were a witchcraft book (actually, it is), and we called Cimeies a "Tincture for Bravery and Expanding the Mind" the recipe would be: drink ½ ounce of whiskey with a drop of red wine vinegar added.

This recipe could be telling the spiritual aspirant to relax, learn everything they can, and to have courage and discipline at the beginning of their alchemical journey. Or perhaps this is a formula that could be added at the beginning of every alchemical process. If you follow the ritual instructions for the Ars Goetia, you should technically be looking into the triangle, into the black mirror while you take your *medicine*. Bottoms up!

As a subtext to this – Cimeies could be a warning to be disciplined when drinking, and to not overdo it, too. It's food for thought.

67: Amduscias

DUKE

Color: Green
Incense: Sandalwood
Metal: Copper
Planet: Venus
Element: Air
(also Amducius and Amdusias)

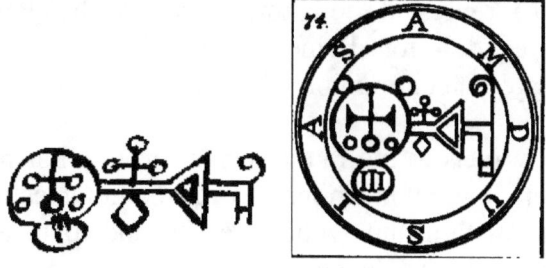

*The 67th spirit in order is called **Amduscias**. He is a strong and great duke appearing at first like a unicorn. But afterwards, at the request of the exorcist, he stands before him in human shape causing trumpets and all manner of musical instruments to be heard but not seen - causing trees to bend and incline according to the exorcist's will. He gives excellent familiars and rules 29 legions of spirits.*

The Alchemical Breakdown:

The seal of Amduscias looks like some kind of distillation apparatus to me. Within it are the symbols for copper (hence Venus), air, a retort used in distillation, fimus equinus (horse dung), vapor, a distillation apparatus, gold, fire, iron, antimony or gold-colored copper alloys, and potentially the aurum potable (drinkable gold).

When we break it down, copper symbolizes the transformation. Air brings clarity and the breath of life. The retort represents the quest for enlightenment and bridging the material and ethereal realms. The horse dung represents earthly matter and the grounding force in which we can sow the seeds of transformation. The vapor represents the veil between worlds, or the unseen. The distillation apparatus represents the crucible of transformation, where chaos births clarity. Gold is the ultimate perfection. is the catalyst for change and transformation. Iron represents grounding and stability. Antimony – or gold-colored alloys of copper – represent the harmonization of the elements or act as a conduit for divine energy. The Aurum Potable could suggest a communion with the divine.

This really feels to me like a recipe for an elixir meant to make spirit communication, or even communication with the divine within and without, easier and to balance the elements within the alchemist.

In the description – the Unicorn symbolizes mercurial forces – the transformative substance that makes transmutation possible. The Unicorn is also associated with the alchemist encountering his shadow self. The tree anchors us to the material world whereas the branches reach into the higher realms. The fact that the description suggests the alchemist can control the trees suggests Amduscias can help the alchemist reach the higher realms while still being rooted firmly in the material world. In western alchemy, trumpets were said to herald alchemical transformations and symbolize communication with higher realms. Other musical instruments might suggest that the melodies of music can evoke higher states of consciousness.

I am convinced by all of this in that I am correct to think that Amduscias is a recipe for a tincture to facilitate communication with the higher self, as well as the divine and celestial beings in other realms.

68: Belial

KING

Color: Yellow
Incense: Frankincense
Metal: Gold
Planet: Sun
Element: Fire (Earth)

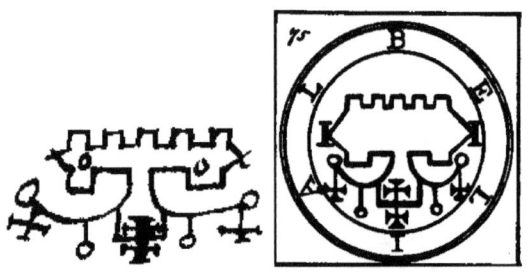

The 68th spirit is called **Belial**. *He is a mighty king and powerful. He was created next after Lucifer and is of his order. He appears in the form of a beautiful angel sitting in a chariot of fire, speaking with a comely voice, declaring that he fell first and amongst the worthier and wiser sort which went before Michael and other heavenly angels. His office is to distribute preferments of senatorships, and to cause favor of friends and foes. He gives excellent familiars and governs 80 legions of spirits. Note this king, Belial, must have offerings, sacrifices, and gifts presented to him by the exorcist or else he will not give true answers to his demands; But then he tarries not one hour in the truth except he be constrained by divine power.*

The Alchemical Breakdown:

My notes on Belial say this: He is a circulating fire. Through clear thought and hard work, you increase your good fortune. The offerings, sacrifices, and gifts are of time and the materials of earth (or the bad habits, thoughts, and feelings we need offer up or sacrifice)– to the fire (active principle).

In the seal itself we have the symbols for acid/vinegar, to mix or meld, lead (Saturn = hard work), metallic mercury (thinking), tin (Jupiter = luck), gold, day, copper, filtration, spiritus (or sublimation), ignis circulatoris (circulating fire), and a clay vessel.

If we look at each of these ingredients alchemically: vinegar purifies the soul through the inner work. Mixing brings the unity of opposites – a merging of the fixed and the volatile. Lead is the prima materia – the first matter. Lead facilitates spiritual enlightenment. Metallic mercury is adaptable and fluid and guides the soul through transformation of consciousness. Tin balances the solar influences of gold, and lead and brings balance to the alchemist. Gold represents wisdom, illumination, and enlightenment.

In the description, he appears as an angel – a volatile force. Belial also seems to have a bit of baggage with his 'fall' from the celestial realms, perhaps suggesting that to be more successful, you have to leave the past in the past.

I would almost say this feels like a recipe for a tincture of good fortune - for letting go of the habits, thoughts, and emotions holding one back from fulfilling their full potential, and finding success.

69: Decarabia

MARQUIS

Color: Violet
Incense: Jasmine
Metal: Silver
Planet: Moon
Element: Air

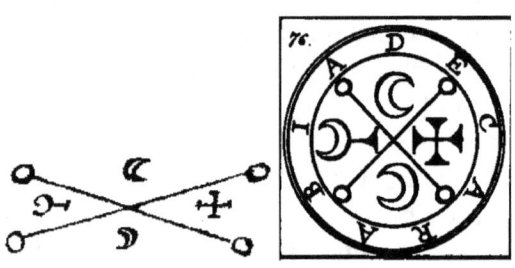

The 69th spirit is called **Decarabia**. He appears in the form of a star in the pentacle at first, but afterwards at the command of the exorcist, he puts on the image of a man. His office is to discover the virtues of herbs and precious stones; and to make the similitude of all birds to fly before the exorcist, and to tarry with him, singing and drinking as natural birds do. He governs 30 legions of spirits, being himself a great marquis.

The Alchemical Breakdown:

This seal contains symbols of the moon, silver, crucibellum (made from bone to purify silver by blowing air across it), and vinegar/acid.

This very much eludes to the process of cupellation – a refining process where an impure metal is melted in a cupel, then a direct blast of hot air on it from a special furnace (or fire assaying) extracts silver from the impure metal. The silver is a byproduct and can be extracted from lead and other mineral ores like copper, gold, and zinc.

As I look deeper into this, it appears that this recipe draws out one's intuition and uses it to understand the natural world and the divine, and to use that intuition to commune with the divine.

I say this because not only do birds, found in the description, represent personal transformation, but they are messengers and mediators between the earthly and heavenly realms. Birds can be messengers of the gods. This suggests the seal of Decarabia is for an alchemical formula or elixir to commune with the divine and to understand the divine nature of all things. To connect to the whole of the natural world and be one with it in perfect harmony and understanding. For spiritual alchemy, it requires the alchemist to extract the part of themselves that reflects its own divine nature in order to draw the same. This means separating the pure from the impure in order to transform the alchemist into an enlightened and intuitive conduit to the natural world.

70: Seere

PRINCE

Color: Blue
Incense: Cedar
Metal: Tin
Planet: Jupiter
Element: Air (Fire)

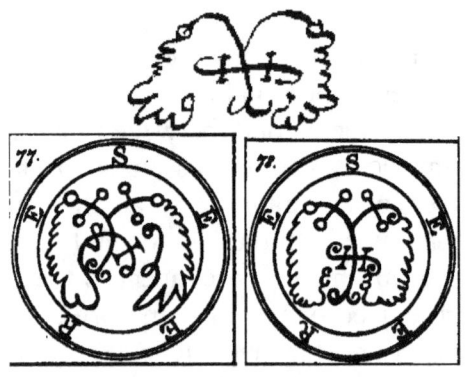

*The 70th spirit in order is called **Seere**. He is a mighty prince and powerful under Amaymon, king of the East. He appears in the form of a beautiful man, riding on a strong horse with wings. His office is to go and come, and to bring all things to pass suddenly, and to carry and recarry anything where you will have it or have it from. For he can pass over the whole world in the twinkling of an eye. He makes a true relation of all sorts of theft and of treasures hidden, and of all other things he is indifferent. Good natured, willing to do anything the Exorcist desires; he governs 26 legions of spirits.*

The Alchemical Breakdown:

The alchemical symbols in this seal include Tin (Jupiter), gold (possibly aqua vitae), one ounce, mosaic silver – a compound of tin used to gild metals, vinegar (could also be cuprum cintrinum – or gold-colored alloys of copper), a strong fire, and possibly arsenic sulfide.

I feel strongly this may have been a recipe to make gilded metals. To put on a façade to make the plain look more polished and therefore more desirable.

Now let's move to the description – he appears as a beautiful man riding upon a strong horse (the four elements and balance) with wings (bringing ascension). His office appears to be that he comes and goes, and things happen, and to toil by carrying things to and fro. Which describes the function of nature. It simply is. Life just happens. This feels almost like day-to-day happenings, or it could be a message to bring the spiritual to your daily toil and find the treasure in your day-to-day mundane life. Uniting the mundane with the spirit. All of the ingredients in the seal point to this being an accurate assessment of the seal. Gold signifies enlightenment, fire and vinegar could suggest breaking down barriers, arsenic sulfide could represent spiritual illumination and the dangers one could face to achieve it, while the mosaic silver could be symbolic of bridging the earthly and celestial realms.

The theft and treasures hidden could be referring to the process of gilding metal. You can hide imperfections through gilding, and perhaps gain more from hiding those imperfections – even though it's likely theft if you're charging premium price for something that is fake. For example, gilding a copper box so that it appears to be gold, and then selling it as gold. It could also symbolize the spiritual person hiding in plain sight, or the unspiritual, gilded in spirituality, pretending to be something they're not. In this case, it could also be a warning to beware of false spiritual teachers.

71: Dantalion

DUKE

Color: Green
Incense: Sandalwood
Metal: Copper
Planet: Venus
Element: Water

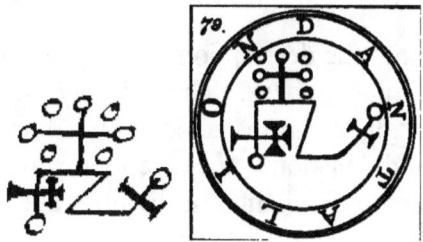

*The 71st spirit is called **Dantalion**. He is a great and mighty duke appearing in the form of a man with many faces, all like men and women, and a book in his right hand. His office is to teach all arts and sciences to anyone, and to declare the secret counsel of anyone, for he knows the thoughts of all men and women and can change them at his will. He can cause love and show by vision the true similitude of anyone let them be in with place or part of the world they will. He governs 36 legions of spirits.*

The Alchemical Breakdown:

I feel like Dantalion encompasses education, knowledge, and wisdom. There also seems to be a glamour aspect to this spirit where it can sway people's opinions and thoughts likely through education. Let's see if the alchemy agrees.

Within the seal we have the symbols for distilled vinegar, a copper vessel, Venus (copper), day, and common salt (sodium chloride). This is, literally, the recipe for creating Verdigris. You could also use this recipe to shine copper.

Copper can be a conduit to connect to the higher self. Vinegar purifies the spirit, dissolves the dirt, and heals. Salt represents earth and cleanses/purifies. Verdigris indicates renewal and the inner work the alchemists must do. From the seal alone, it almost looks like a recipe for spiritual purification.

Now let's look at the description. He appears as the form of a man with many faces. This simply suggests he is "everyman" and he carries a book which can symbolize knowledge and wisdom, the Hermetic tradition, inner alchemy, laboratory alchemy, or the Emerald Tablet itself.

I agree with both of my thoughts about the seal and the description. Dantalion brings knowledge of the inner alchemical work and spiritual purification, both of which can help us understand the nature and habits of others as well as ourselves, and can be used to sway the beliefs of others through sharing of education and knowledge.

72: Andromalius

EARL

Color: Red
Incense: Dragon's Blood
Metal: Copper or Silver
Planet: Mars
Element: Fire

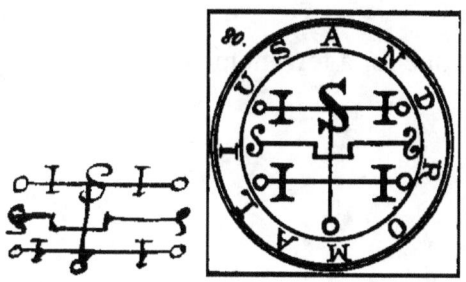

*The 72nd spirit in order is called **Andromalius**. He is a great and mighty earl appearing in the form of a man, holding a serpent in his hand. His office is to bring a thief and goods stolen, back. And to discover all wickedness, and underhanded dealings, and to punish thieves and other wicked people. He also discovers treasure that is hidden. He rules 36 legions of spirits.*

The Alchemical Breakdown:

In this seal are the symbols for sulfur, iron, copper, silver, day, dry, and filter (which could be distillation). This appears to be a recipe to create the "Oil of Vitriol" or a liquid sulfuric acid that would then be allowed to dry and crystallize, creating sulfuric acid crystals or crystalized oil of vitriol. The process of making the oil of vitriol symbolizes the inner journey of the alchemist including purification, dissolution, and the union of opposites. It brings with it hidden wisdom and divine revelation.

Andromalius, in his description, also brings hidden wisdom and divine revelation – the treasure - in the serpent that he carries in his hand. The description of his office is a heavy metaphor. The thief is all the things in life (and within us) that steal our joy or peace. Andromalius can bring such things back and can help you remove (destroy) those things in your life (and inner self) that rob you of a more spiritual and peaceful existence.

Sit with this one for a few moments.

Other Grimoires

Clavis Inferni: Grimoire of St. Cyprian

Sadly, the sigils of the four kings of the Ars Goetia are not included in the Ars Goetia. The Clavis Inferni, a late 18th century manuscript, does have the seals of the four kings, but they are not of the same style as the seals of the Ars Goetia, showing that they were, in fact, created later by a different author who abandoned the alchemical seals in favor of traditional pictorial emblems and a series of cyphers, alongside Hebrew characters and Gematria.

The 4 Goetic Kings in Ars Goetia include Egyn (also sometimes listed as Zimimar), Uriens (also sometimes listed as Amaymon), Maymon (also sometimes listed as Corson), and Paymon (also sometimes listed as Gaap). The emblems have alchemical symbolism and color messages, as well as Hebrew characters which are important in gematria, which often goes hand in hand with alchemical work. But there is a distinct absence of the same alchemical symbol-based seals. Instead, the Clavis Inferni seems to have its own cypher set. You can read more about this in *The Grimoire of St. Cyprian - Clavis Inferni* (Sourceworks of Ceremonial Magic) by Dr Stephen Skinner and David Rankine, Llewellyn Publications; Illustrated Hardcover edition (September 8, 2010).

You can see these seals in the next image and notice just how different they are.

The Serpent Ouroboros and the seals of the Four Demon Kings.

The upper right is the seal of Urieus (Uriens). Bottom left is the seal of Paymon. Bottom right is Maymon, and the upper left is Egyn.

The Grand Grimoire and the Grimoirium Verum

Perhaps two of the more famous grimoires are The Grand Grimoire and the Grimorium Verum. The Grimoirium Verum is where you'll find the sigils of the 9 principal spirits found in both of these grimoires. The Grimoirium Verum was allegedly written in 1517, which means it's slightly earlier than the Ars Goetia. If this is, in fact, true, then it feels as though the use of alchemy in these sigils is a bit more rudimentary, or in some cases, very selective. There are no seals in any of the copies of the Grand Grimoire that I have. The seals are, however, in most copies of The Grimoirium Verum, which adds an additional 18 spirits and their sigils. I have included a lot of the seals here so you can see how they differ, suggesting again a different authorship. That said, you can pick out some of the alchemical symbols with just a cursory glance. I will leave most of these seals for you to go decode on your own. It's always a good exercise for the magician or alchemist to try something for him or herself. By reading it, you simply know it. By doing it, you experience it and can understand it. Consider it more homework.

I am going to include some of my observations for some of the seals on the following pages for your consideration.

Lucifer, Beelzebuth, and Astaroth all have a ring of seals enveloping seals inside the circle. They also contain characters outside the initial emblems. You can easily pick out some of the alchemical symbols.

Lucifer: Aqua Vitae, water, spiritus (alcohol), talcum or vinegar, calcination, common salt, and crucible. This pretty much deciphers the seal of Lucifer on the bottom right – the one that most Luciferians or Satanists use for Lucifer. The character on the left includes the symbol for water and the sun.

Beelzebuth – in the inner circle we have some kind of transformation of lead going on, while in the outer circle the immediate symbols I pick out are the symbols for a solution or solvent, salt, and tin (Jupiter).

Astaroth – In this emblem I was able to quickly pick out the symbols for saltpeter, lead (Saturn), and distillation.

There are many more alchemical symbols here. What can

you find?

Here are three characters of Lucifer, outside his circle:

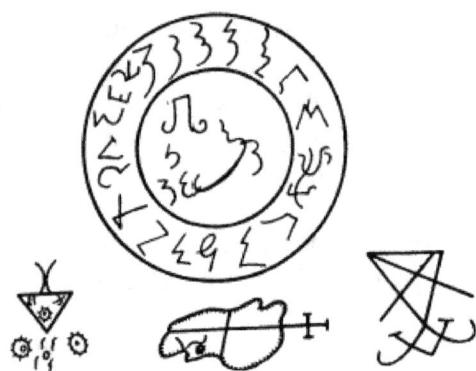

The following are those of Beelzebuth and Astaroth placed outside their circles:

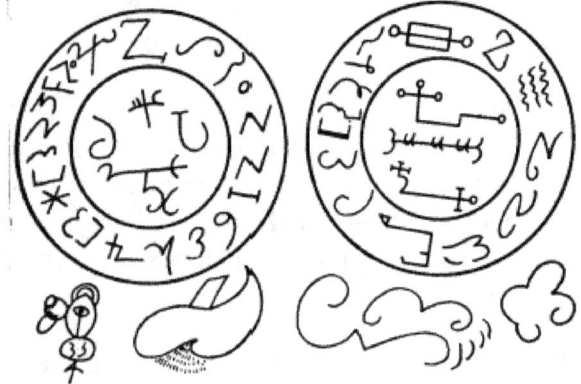

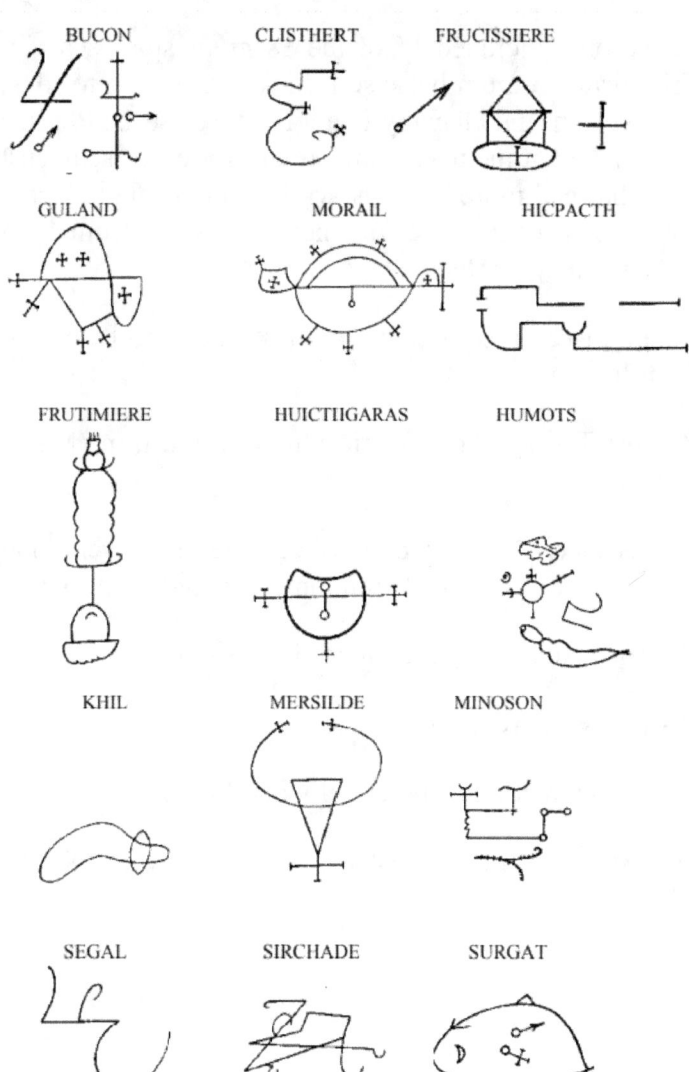

I have only included 15 of the 18 *other* spirit seals in the Grimoirium Verum because I think it's enough to illustrate how we can find alchemy in a lot of these seals. Please note that I have not included commentary for every seal. Just the ones that had more obvious symbolism. Though, I have no doubt that every one of these seals is teeming with alchemical symbolism.

Again, just a cursory glance at these seals and I can tell you the following:

Bucon: The symbols for tin (Jupiter) and iron (Mars) are present.

Frucissiere: The symbols for steel/iron, acid/vinegar, autumn, fire, water, and antimony prepared spagyrically.

Guland: Acid/vinegar abounds in this one.

Huitiigaras: Acid and arsenic.

Mersilde: Water and potentially distillation.

Surgat: The moon (Silver), Mars (Iron), and Venus (Copper)

Here is a more in depth look at **Frucissiere** as an example of how we could read this seal:

Frucissiere in his description is said to bring the dead to life. He is fire and Mars but also indicative of all the elements in the earth (iron). Notice the mars/iron and acid/vinegar (a primary component is most alchemical transmutations of metal) symbols above. Along with the triangular symbols for Fire and Water. The combination of fire and water symbolizes autumn and a spagyric preparation, and the house shape is a symbol for antimony, a brittle, silvery-like metalloid. From this sigil alone we can make an educated guess that maybe Mars is the planetary correspondent, iron is the metal, and this spirit's purpose is about tempering emotions and balancing the magician. And since Frucissuere is a Death Daemonic (one of the many Daemons worked with in necromancy) it would stand to reason that Frucissiere can ease grief (tempering emotions) and bring the dead back for a short while as with necromancy. From the earth, to the ethereal by way of grief? You may have your own interpretation of this.

Planetary Seals of Solomon

As I was finishing up this book, I was glancing through the planetary seals for another project and the alchemical symbols within the planetary seals were jumping out at me. Once you see it, you can't unsee it and it will open a whole new perspective to you. As you go through all of the Solomonic texts, and the earlier grimoires, look at the emblems and you will begin to see it, too.

Conclusion

This brings me to the conclusion of this book. These grimoires were written by men, not spirits. If they started out as spiritual texts – they started as unverified personal gnosis (UPG) backed by personal observations and experimentations. It was up to other alchemists to test, observe, and experience this gnosis through practice of the recipes and to verify the information for themselves. Because the books survived for so long, they became canon for ceremonial magicians, but sadly the symbol keys, which may have been standard knowledge among medieval alchemists, survived separately alongside the grimoires and likely weren't entirely linked unless one studied with alchemists who knew better.

My conclusion is this: The Ars Goetia and many other grimoires are the cypher-filled journals of an alchemist or group of alchemists, detailing experiments in both spiritual and laboratory alchemy. The symbols used in Ars Goetia are from the relevant period in which the books manifested, suggesting they were not written any earlier than the medieval era.

Men are fallible. These books weren't channeled by gods. They were created by human hands. They were encoded with cyphers by human brains. They are a testament to early psychology and the precursor to chemistry.

In the context of magick, I couldn't help but think that the seals in the Ars Goetia are basically magickal programs that execute when we utilize the symbol in our magick provided we understand what the symbols mean. They activate the alchemical spiritual processes described within them.

Which makes me feel like, in actuality, the program activates an egregore created by centuries of magicians who have placed their own anthropomorphic expectations on the egregore. Because at this point – I'm pretty sure the use of pagan god-names (or variants), place names, or made-up names has more to do with gematria, which is another book. Then again – as within, so without. As above, so below.

That said – I suppose we can't deny that these spirits, these egregores, become our personalized thought forms (this even happens with god-forms) and are therefore very valid in the context of our personal gnosis, too. Because the original Goetic spirits weren't actually spirits, but rather names associated with recipes, ideas, concepts, or spells if you prefer, for both spiritual/metaphysical and sometimes even laboratory alchemy; and the original authors of the grimoires were alchemists, psychologists, and philosophers, and magick was both the shadow work (psychology) involved in the betterment of the self, and the precursor to the sciences of metallurgy and chemistry.

But, over the centuries, for a lot of people the alchemy was lost, and the Ars Goetia became this mystical, mythical, and magickal text in its own right. All because we need to label and classify things and put them into neat little boxes. We've separated the branches of Western Magick which were never meant to separated. They're all interconnected and if you don't understand one part, you won't understand the other. I've been saying this for years.

I look forward to other authors continuing to add to my work here and potentially spending time to decode other grimoires in the same way to further the discussion on how western alchemy and the symbol keys played a central role in medieval grimoires.

I do hope this book has offered some insight and perspective into the Ars Goetia and inspires you, my fellow magicians and alchemists. Thank you for reading.

Bibliography and Suggested Reading

76 Week Goetia, S. Connolly, 2023, DB Publishing/Darkerwood Publishing Group

Alchemical Symbols Edited by Adam McLean, 2017, Independently Published.

Alchemical Symbols Fourth Edition by Philip Wheeler, 2018, R.A.M.S. Publishing Company

Alchemy: Science of the Cosmos, Science of the Soul by Titus Burckhardt, 1997, Fons Vitae

Daemonolatry Goetia, S. Connolly, 2010, DB Publishing

Dictionary of the Occult, Hermetic, and Alchemical Sigils by Fred Gettings - 1981 Routledge & Kegan Paul Ltd, London. Currently out of print but also available as a free PDF on a lot of esoteric archive websites.

Medicinisch chymisch und alchemistisches Oraculum - 1755

Occult Symbolism of Animals, Insects, Reptiles, Fish and Birds by Manley P. Hall, 2019, Lamp of Trismegistus

Practical Alchemy: A Guide to the Great Work by Brian Cotnoir, 2021, Weiser Books (Previously The Weiser Concise Guide to Alchemy by Brian Cotnoir, 2006, Weiser Books)

Real Alchemy: A Primer of Practical Alchemy by Robert Allen Bartlett, 2009, Ibis Press (3rd Revised Edition)

Splendor Solis - Salomon Trismosin. Many translations and free versions are available.

The Grimoire of St. Cyprian - Clavis Inferni (Sourceworks of Ceremonial Magic) by Dr Stephen Skinner and David Rankine, 2010, Llewellyn Publications; Illustrated Hardcover edition.

The Golden Work or ***The Golden Treatise of Hermes*** - Hermes Trismegistus. Numerous translations are available and you should be able to find this online.

The Hermetic and Alchemical Writings - Paracelsus. There are numerous translations available and you should be able to find this online for free.

The Lesser Key of Solomon edited by Joseph Peterson, 2001, Weiser Books. ***The Ars Goetia*** is also available online at esotericarchives.com

Acknowledgements

I have a lot of people to thank in this one because, as I always say, no book is born in a vacuum. In the 2+ years it took me to put this together, through to that final push, there were so many people who offered their help and resources, or just listened as I bounced ideas off them. First, thank you to my husband, Matt, who, whenever inspiration strikes, makes sure I have the time to work and makes sure that I eat. I am sometimes so possessed by my Daemons and their inspiration that I forget things like eating.

To my friend, Shae, my partner in crime and sister from another mister, for always listening when things get challenging and giving me an objective ear and a word of encouragement when I need it.

My friend, Amanda, graciously offered her help with anything I needed. Amanda is another one who let me bounce ideas off her at all hours and found time to squeeze me in despite being a busy mom and wife, magician, and running her own business. I don't know if words can appropriately express my gratitude.

A shout out to my editor, Mike, as well. Not only has he been another sounding board and someone to bounce ideas off of, but he also makes time to look at pages as I go. Plus, if I ever called him and told him I needed help, he wouldn't ask questions. It would be – what do you need, sis?

And to everyone else who beta read, discussed alchemy with me at length, and cheered me on with this one including Connie, Corrine, Ken, Tiffany, Frank, Jennifer, and SO many other people (you know who you are) who took time out of their busy lives to offer information, opinions, a kind word, or advice, or to tell me to keep going -- you all mean the world to me.

About the Author

Bestselling author S. Connolly has been practicing and studying all things "occult" and metaphysical since 1984. Her interest started with divination, gematria, and necromancy and quickly spiraled toward ceremonial magick, witchcraft, and Daemons. She has been a practicing Daemonolatress since 1988 and is the author of *The Complete Book of Daemonolatry*, *Keys of Ocat*, *76 Week Goetia*, and many more. She also writes occult fiction as Audrey Brice, steamy dark romance as Anne O'Connell, and she writes PG 13 fiction as S. J. Reisner.

For more information about the author or demonolatry see: www.demonolatry.org or www.sjreisner.com

www.ingramcontent.com/pod-product-compliance
Lightning Source LLC
LaVergne TN
LVHW011947060526
838201LV00061B/4239